Mainstay Press publishes books geared to social change, along with other political books – fiction and nonfiction both. Mainstay books help readers understand the realities and possibilities of contemporary social and political life – the life of the public that is profoundly related to the personal lives of people everywhere.

POINT OF NO RETURN

More praises for Point of No Return

"A fascinating look at the world through the eyes of a war correspondent – a world few of us know."
- ***Eve Jackson (France24)***

"An exhilarating wallop of a novel that flattens quite a few *idées reçues.* "- ***Thierry Ménétrier (Paris Normandie)***

"This book is an extraordinary testimonial to the end of the 20th century and the life of a man who is both humble and altogether exceptional (in his approach to existence, the positions he takes and the life that he leads), as well as that of his contemporaries. A heavy favourite! "
- ***www.laculturesepartage.over-blog.com***

"A serious piece of writing endowed with great sincerity, portraying a unique life experience that leaves us feeling forlorn even as it pulls us along in its wake."
- ***Nathalie Zylberman - Vallée FM***

"Once again, it's the context that makes the book. It is quite simply mind-boggling. Andre Vltchek knows very well what he's talking about (...). It is a book that cannot fail to move, a rich, strong and dense tale, by all means get a hold of a copy for an intelligent read!" - ***Yves Mabon***

"An instructive and brilliant book that forces the reader to face the question: What sort of world are we leaving to our children? How could we ever justify ourselves? How far are we willing to go to change it?" - ***Valérie Revelut***

"Quite simply a masterpiece... All of the absurdity of our society, its lack of humanity and sense blows up in our face... All readers will feel touched by this narrative that speaks of liberty, choice and our place in the world."- ***Stephanie Morelli***

"A splendid novel that will leave no one cold. The author skilfully takes us along on a mysterious and sorrowful journey. A gripping read. " - ***Patrick Martinez - Radio Coteaux***

"A searching look at weighty questions on man and his destructive and at the same time rebellious proclivities, on the role of information, on the intoxication of an engagement that is also heart-rending and paradoxical for this great reporter. Vibrant!" - ***Luc Monge - La Savoie***

"Part fiction, part autobiography, this book recounts the life story of a great reporter, the kind who takes risks to get a story or a photo spread while so many of his colleagues make their fortune filling up the gossip pages of magazines. It's the grandeur and poverty of journalism. " - ***Roland Françoise***

"André Vltchek offers an unsparing portrait of the world we live in. With his provocative outlook, he lays bare a situation that is really quite simple, and did not begin yesterday... Although this book does not raise easy questions, it is indeed easy to read, thanks to the wit and subtlety of its author. " - ***Françoise Bachelet***

"This book is teeming with reflections on our modern world. It raises questions on violence and war, but also on political strategy and the suffering of the ordinary people who put up with it all... It is a most instructive book, and one that allows for a better understanding of international politics. One thing is for certain; a trip around the world in 374 pages is too good a deal to turn down." - ***Column by Iluze***

POINT OF NO RETURN

Andre Vltchek

Mainstay Press
Imaginative Literature and Social Change

This book is a work of fiction. All characters are fictional.

Published by
Mainstay Press

First edition, 2005
Second edition, 2007
Third edition, 2013

Cover photo by Alejandro Wagner Molina: the World Trade Center prior to 9-11-2001.

ISBN: 978-0-9774590-7-0

Mis pasos en esta calle
Resuenan
En otra calle
Donde
Oigo mis pasos
Pasar en esta calle
Donde
Solo es real la niebla.

Octavio Paz

The sun shone, having no alternative, on the nothing new.

Samuel Beckett

PART I

1

A Palestinian man stood in the middle of a dusty road in Rafah refugee camp. Next to him stood his donkey. The man was old and so was the donkey.

Israelis fired air-to-ground missiles from helicopters. The earth shook while the old man stood in the middle of the road, blissfully indifferent to what was happening around him.

I liked his face. It was a good face, covered by wrinkles, not very expressive but good nevertheless. I took photographs of him and then we stood there, looking at each other. I greeted him in English and in Arabic and he answered though we knew there could be no serious conversation between us. We belonged to different worlds. I had come to learn and to see and to write, while he was here to stay.

He was a gentle man – it was obvious from the way he treated his donkey...stroking its mane, resting the palm of his hand on the animal's neck. Donkeys in Gaza pulled old overloaded two-wheel carts and they looked exhausted, overworked and hungry. The old man did not use his donkey for anything in particular, it was simply his companion. It was easy to sell donkeys in Gaza – even old animals were put to work. But these two were used to each other: an old man and his beast.

We walked together for a few minutes. They were my silent guides in Rafah refugee camp. We did not try to speak, the surroundings were explicit enough, no need for words. I took several rolls of film while they watched me working. We spotted small stalls on a sidewalk and I stopped and ordered two cups of tea. The weather was hot and humid.

When two Israeli helicopters approached from the North and flew above the camp, the old man pointed toward the sky and smiled sadly. Even when new explosions thundered on the edge of town, he did not seem scared. Neither was his donkey.

I wanted to give him something as a token of my friendship, but there were only films, light meters, notebooks and pencils in the pockets of my jacket. I found a small photograph in my wallet and after some hesitation handed it to him. He looked at the image very attentively and then smiled.

It was a picture of the ancient city of Nara in autumn, full of powerful colors, serenity and peace. An eight-year-old Japanese girl stood next to the entrance of a small shrine holding the hand of her mother, a woman with a sad smile, long black hair and a beautiful though pale face. The girl was laughing at the camera, her long white scarf falling to one side, almost touching the ground.

"No war?" asked the old man.
"No," I said.

"Good," he said. "Good that it is still there...the world outside."

He held the picture between his fingers. His hands were rough.

"May Allah be with them." He began to hand the picture back to me.

"Keep it," I said.

We shook hands, and I boarded the car, asking my driver to wait. I watched the man and his donkey. They slowly disappeared into the crowd. Surrounded by hopelessness and despair, the old man and his animal seemed surprisingly calm. Both were too old to expect a better future. Both had been stripped of the ability to desire and dream.

In the middle of the intifada, in a time of hate and constant death, both the man and the animal seemed happy.

2

Professor Kohn cleaned his glasses with the stained table cloth. He downed his beer and ordered another bottle. We were in a Yemeni dive, underground, somewhere in Jerusalem, after La Belle closed at midnight. Tonight there were no women accompanying Kohn. As far as I could remember, this was the first time he had come alone.

"What the color is God?" he asked.

I had no clue. I had never met God and I had no idea whether He planned to meet me. I had never given a thought to what color He might be. Or to whether He had any color. I had no idea even whether He existed or not.

"Does He have a color?" I wondered. "He could be as colorless as He is shapeless."

"Blue," said Kohn. "He may be blue, or He may be green. What if He is blue?"

"I don't know," I said. "That would be quite agreeable. Blue is not bad."

The Yemeni dive consisted of several tables and wet walls. It was an illegal gambling den, one of those places where Kohn liked to conclude his excessive drinking escapades. It was hot and humid, smoky and loud.

"They are killing each other again, because of God," continued Kohn. "As they have been killing each other for centuries and millennia. Christians killing pagans, Muslims killing North Africans, then Christians killing Muslims and Muslims killing Christians. Later Hindus killing Muslims and Muslims killing Hindus, while Christians killed everybody they found in their way. Then Muslims killing Muslims: Shiites killing Sunnis and vice versa. Catholics killing Protestants and vice versa. Catholics and Protestants killing Jews. Jews killing Muslims and Muslims killing infidels."

"It doesn't seem that Jews are killing now because of God," I suggested.

"They are. You bet they are. Maybe not because of their own God, but because they don't like the way others see Him."

"Or Her," I added.

"Exactly. Or Her. There is hardly any war that isn't fought on behalf of God. Anyway, I would like to ask them if they know what color He may be. They are all convinced that they know Him, can identify the One through whom He spoke. But they don't even know His color. That's strange."

"Very strange," I agreed, drinking my watered-down *uzo*.

"I wonder how He can stand it – all that killing in His name. Takes guts, doesn't it? The Nazis used to say '*Gott mit uns*' before butchering half of Europe. Before dropping their idiotic smart bombs, American leaders never forget their 'God Bless America.' You know what Pakistanis do when they fire shells at Indian positions? Instead of 'Fire!' they scream 'God is great!' And then 'pah!'"

I looked around. A young woman with heavy gold bracelets served colorful food. Tourist posters depicting the Sinai desert hung on the walls. Faded paint on the ceiling.

"Kohn," I said. "I've had enough. I have to go back to my hotel. I have to cover that mess outside, tomorrow."

"So what will you write about this time?" he asked.

"I don't know. Whatever comes my way. Whatever happens."

"Whatever you write about, don't ever forget that none of them knows anything significant. They all pretend that they know..."

"Kohn," I said, exhausted. "They just want their land back."

"That part is probably true," he admitted. "And they should get it back. But they should want it in the name of simple justice, not in the name of something about which they don't even know the color."

I had no desire to be here. Five years ago I would have gone to any place on earth, as long as there was something worth writing about. Now I had become picky. Wars were repetitive, after all, and so was the suffering of people who had to live through them. I was getting profoundly bored with wars. I had written and reported from every corner of the globe for more than ten years. I had written books. Put together documentaries. Nothing changed. The same outbursts of insane violence, the same burned houses, bombed cities, women in tears kneeling in the middle of devastated streets, hospitals out of medicine and blood and bandages.

As I was crossing the Rafah border to the Egyptian Sinai, I tried not to look at the depressing Israeli and Egyptian watchtowers and high voltage electric wires. The new Gaza airport had been closed because of the uprising, and my airplane ticket to Cairo was now worth nothing more than the paper on which it was printed.

I bribed the driver of a tourist bus loaded with frightened Japanese tourists to secure a smoking seat in the first row, and as the bus moved, I watched with profound indifference the straight road ahead, cutting through the monotonous dunes of the Sinai Desert.

*

I tried to recall recent events.

Two days earlier, right after I had left Kohn, I watched Israeli soldiers regrouping on the square next to the Wailing Wall. It was late at night. Thirty of them formed a circle, receiving last orders from their commander who happened to be a young and pretty girl in her early twenties.

Sounds of gunfire were coming clearly from the other side of the wall, from the Muslim part, from which the illuminated dome of the Temple of the Rock penetrated a dark and cloudless sky over the city of Jerusalem.

The Israeli soldiers were young and some of them were scared. I saw one of them cover his nose with his hand and there was blood running between his fingers. His friends noticed and offered water from their bottles and patted his back, saying something encouraging in Hebrew that I could not understand.

I took several photographs of the soldiers, of police vans that blocked all entrances to the square, of the mosque behind the wall, and finally of the girl commander. I took her picture when the wind picked up her dark hair, fully uncovering her face and she smiled and I lowered my camera and we looked at each other for a few seconds. We were standing in the middle of the deserted square, in the middle of the Holy City of Jerusalem, right in front of the Wailing Wall. There were green lights illuminating the Dome of the Rock and the moon and the stars above looked almost unreal and then I heard shots again, coming from the other side. I liked the girl and she smiled at me, but then she lowered her eyes and raised them again, but this time she looked straight ahead, at her men who stood around her as she said something in Hebrew, that harsh and beautiful language I had always wanted to comprehend, and the men formed ranks and walked away toward the bridge, toward the passage leading to the Dome of the Rock, toward the gunshots, the sporadic explosions and screams. I followed with my eyes until they were gone.

I looked around and the *mosque* was still there and so was the Jewish wall. The Israeli girl soldier with black hair falling on her uniform was gone. I lit up a cigarette and thought about her for a while, about her firm breasts that I could sense under her blouse. I tried to imagine how she would look when she wore light summer sandals instead of heavy boots.

I felt sad, imagining that she might be getting screwed while I was lying on my bed reading Celine, but I had no intentions of going there, of going to the other side. I'd had them all up to here and I had seen all of it so many times that I really had no curiosity left, tonight. They would be hiding behind several corners next to the Dome of the Rock, shooting rubber-coated bullets into a crowd of rock-throwing Palestinians. Once in a while they would lose their temper and shoot real bullets and there would be blood on the cobblestones.

I walked through the deserted old city toward Dan Gate and Jaffa Street, passing dark and narrow alleys and closed doors of shops. She'd had beautiful eyes but then many girls in the world had beautiful eyes – I wondered whether women's feet also stink when they are squeezed for ten hours in heavy military boots. I wondered whether she was scared, whether she had doubts, whether she felt sorrow. I hoped that night that she would not get killed. I hoped she would not kill that night.

The next day at four o'clock in the afternoon Israeli helicopters flew over Erez Checkpoint, spraying the main highway of Gaza with bullets and rockets, hitting cars, and destroying the dilapidated dwellings of refugees. The Strip exploded in massive spontaneous protests and there was fighting next to the road and Palestinian ambulances rushed through the abandoned streets of Gaza City with their sirens howling, wheels throwing dust.

I spent the entire morning in the burning center of Hebron on the West Bank, then crossed at Erez Checkpoint to the Strip early in the afternoon. Suddenly it was here again: one of the most hopeless places on earth, that filthy and dusty concentration of human misery – Gaza City.

I took photographs of the barricades, of fires and helicopters and then of wounded men being carried to ambulances. In just one hour my shoes and jeans were covered by dust and my face was sweaty and burned, and I had to clean my camera lenses and glasses every ten minutes.

The headquarters of the UNRWA was empty, almost everybody was frantically working in the field. I went straight to Shifa Hospital.

A silent crowd of Palestinians stood in front of the main gate – mostly young women and old men – and I pushed my way to the emergency room, passing by countless volunteers, nurses and doctors, changing films as I went, changing lenses and attaching the flash gun, still sweating and swearing in the devilish heat.

I bumped into stretchers covered with blood – blood on the floor tiles, on walls, everywhere. I heard someone screaming and I went straight to the surgery room and there was a Palestinian man on the bed, his face twisted by pain, naked and hairy and wounded in the stomach. Next to him, separated by the plastic curtain howled another man, his penis erect and blue, dark blue and red, his balls looked crushed, two doctors covered it all with medicine. The man had been hit by rubber bullets. The doctors injected something into his arm but he kept screaming and four male nurses had to pin him down while somebody pushed me inside and yelled: "Take pictures of this – take pictures of what they are doing to our people," and I took some twenty photos, but only of the man's face and then I took the entire roll of film of another man behind the curtain covered by blood and of exhausted faces of doctors and nurses and of all the mess on the floor and on the walls.

Every few minutes ambulances brought new patients to the emergency room, some with gunshot wounds, some burned, some already dead.

I had to get out of the hospital because the stench and heat were unbearable. I thought conditions would be better working on the road between Erez and Rafah, where the real fighting had erupted. Even there I found no breeze, the air was heavy, and the Israeli pilots seemed not to give a shit about anything, shooting at nearly all that moved on the ground while the soldiers switched from rubber bullets to standard ammunition.

I wrote my report at midnight in a bizarre posh beach hotel.

I sat alone at the table overlooking the sea, ready for a late dinner, but when the food arrived I had no desire to eat. My head was heavy, I felt dehydrated and exhausted. I had to get my films to New York.

*

A bus rolled onto the ferry and we crossed the Suez Canal, leaving Asia. Crossing took only five minutes. The African side looked no different: a desert... and a dusty provincial town as a kind of small green oases next to the highway. I had no idea why I was going to Cairo, except that now this was the only way out of Gaza. The bus was going there and the bus was air-conditioned and the driver did not mind my smoking.

3

I waited for her note. I knew she would write. She always did, every day, several times a day.

At the business center of the Hilton Hotel I checked my email. Her message was there, early in the list.

Dear Karel. I'm in Sipan, walking along white beaches at sunset. Alone. I had to escape Tokyo and my work. I need to be by myself. Away from everybody, away from my husband, even from Keiko. Tonight I turned on the TV in my room and I saw news from the Middle East. I watched in horror. I thought I saw you in Gaza. You were wearing a black vest and you had two cameras. I was afraid something might happen to you. They said the Israeli army had been shooting at cars from helicopters. They showed a short clip of a child hiding behind his older brother (or was it his father?). They both were killed. I felt so sad. How can you do this work? There is so much beauty in this world – why do you always have to work where there is no hope and so much pain? I am sure you need a rest, too.

I have convinced the Editor of my magazine that we should use the story about Aswan and Luxor. Since they closed the crossing to Israel, I gather you are now in Egypt, probably in Cairo. You know we pay very well. And there would be no clash of interests with your magazine – this would be a travel story. Can you go? Aswan is only one thousand kilometers from Cairo. The Magazine will pay for your tickets and hotel. You can write a story, a short one, in English and I will translate it to Japanese. Relax, enjoy old Egypt, write something light, take some beautiful photos. Please say yes.

Keiko sends you her greetings. My husband has left Tokyo for two weeks. He has to work in Sapporo. I think about you always.
Reiko

I accepted the offer. At a travel agency I bought a round-trip ticket, first class, on the sleeper train to Aswan.

4

"He is a new Egyptian Picasso," sighed Mahmud, my driver, flashing a monstrosity in front of my eyes, while I sipped Egyptian red wine, and puffed on the water pipe.

"Hell, he is not."

We were in some hole in the wall in old Cairo. Mahmud drank something resembling Turkish coffee, one after the other. I gathered he had never heard about heart attacks and strokes.

"Do you want to see belly dancing?"

"Not tonight," I said.

"By the way, are you Jewish?" he asked.

"No."

"You look like a blonde Jew."

"Kiss my ass, Mahmud." I ordered another glass of heavy and fruity red wine. There was no booze visible. Bottles were fetched from behind the counter, dusty and dubious looking, no labels. As with women in Cairo, they seemed to appear from nowhere.

"I may if you buy two paintings."

"Just looking at them makes me shiver."

"With delight?" he asked hopefully.

"With horror. Do they come from a mental institution? Have you looted the art therapy workshop of an insane asylum?"

"Of course not!" screamed Mahmud, who had been a high school art teacher in Alexandria, before things became confusing after Nasser.

He could have been my grandfather. I had always had good luck with my drivers, once being driven in Sofia by a former Bulgarian Ambassador to the UN.

"Fine, forget about Picasso. Maybe you don't see much of Picasso in there. But you have to admit there is plenty of Chagall. Concentrate on the colors."

He put two unframed paintings on the filthy table: yellow pigs flying over an enormous gray city that did not remotely resemble Vitebsk or Paris.

"Two hundred dollars for each. Last price. Do you like Jews?"

"Sure," I said. "Why not?"

"They kill innocent Palestinian children."

"Mahmud..."

"They kill babies," he repeated. "And you like them. Why?"

"They write good books."

"But they kill babies."

"Mahmud," I said, "everybody kills babies. Muslims kill babies in Sudan and elsewhere, Americans killed babies in Indochina and Latin America, Europeans have killed babies all over the world. Everybody kills babies. It's terrible but it's a fact. Are you obsessed? Are Jews all you can think about? Do you have dreams about them when you sleep?"

"Nightmares," said Mahmud, darkly. "Let's get back to our business. Buy this Arab Chagall and I will throw something into the bargain."

I ordered a coffee for myself. It was aromatic and very strong. One was definitely all I could take.

"What can you throw in?"

"A virgin," he said.

"A *what*?"

"A virgin. A real local virgin."

"No way," I said. "You have to marry one."

"Not necessarily."

"There is no way you can produce a local virgin...unless she is as fake as your Chagall."

"You will see," he smiled demonically.

"Mahmud," I said, "I'm not sure if I want to see anything. I wish I could have a simple Egyptian driver: modest, friendly, honest and punctual. I don't need a virgin. I really don't."

"You are sick," he said. "Such a driver does not exist in Cairo. You will not find one. You need an Egyptian virgin. And don't tell me you don't want one – everybody wants one. Even I want one."

"Mahmud," I said, recalling an old Egyptian proverb, "your words are like the buzzing of flies in my ears."

He drove me to my hotel.

"Good night," I said. "I'm going to sleep."

"You are not," he replied. "Your night will be as great as a volcanic eruption, like the fireworks at the opening of the Sydney Olympic Games, or to bring it closer to home, like a camel's ejaculation. And in the morning you will come to me and say: Mahmud, my friend, I will buy all that great artwork that you have hidden in your cellar because last night you changed my life..."

"Your mother had a hairy chest," I said.

"So what?" he replied. "She was veiled from head to toe, anyway."

At ten o'clock in the evening my phone rang. On the other end of the line I could hear the shaking voice of a receptionist.

"Sir," he said. "Oh sir. There is...a lady. She is looking for you. She is going upstairs. She is very.... Should I stop her? Should I call the police? Should I notify the armed forces?"

But it was too late. A few moments later somebody was knocking on my door in an extremely determined manner.

I opened, she pushed me aside and sailed into the room. All in black, covered from head to toe, walking on needles. I had never seen such high heels before. The woman was almost as monumental as the Dome of the Rock.

"Mahmud sent me," she said through the veil. "I'm your virgin."

"Jesus," I said. I had no idea that they came in this size. Egyptian virgins, especially.

"You killed him," she said.

"What?"

"You killed Jesus."

"Me? When did I kill Jesus?"

"You, I mean, Jews."

I had to have a drink.

"Am I a Jew? Anyway, I thought the Romans killed him..."

"Mahmud said you like them."

"Sit down," I said. "Something to drink?"

"Beer," she said.

"Really?" I looked at her veil. "Is it...allowed? I mean, not that I'm particularly religious..."

"Fine, a glass of water."

She was enormous. Taller than I. She could be...my horse. I wanted her out. I wanted her out desperately. I was ready to pay for her immediate departure.

"Not that I care," I said, downing Stoli straight from a bottle I found in the mini bar. "But are you really a virgin?"

"Yes," she said. "Never fucked before."

"Never what?" I lit up a cigarette.

"Never kissed a boy," she corrected herself.

For some strange reason I had thought that Muslim virgins generally did not swear and did not drink beer with strangers. But maybe I was wrong. Life had proved me wrong on so many occasions.

"I like you, boy," she said and it sounded like a pickup line from the port of Cebu.

"Should I be honored?" I said.

Obviously there was something fishy in all this. As I spoke, I backed up, slowly, toward the door. She came after me. I jumped toward the exit but she had it well planned: she planted her enormous self between me and the door.

"I'm shy," she whispered. "I'll blow you, but please don't undress me."

"I won't," I promised. "I won't undress you."

"Come here, baby," she said. I noticed she had a strange accent.

Shit, I thought. No emergency exit. No stick to hit her over the head with. She was almost twice my size.

"Can't we just sit down and talk about the Palestinian conflict and the sanctions against Iraq?" I offered.

"Later," she said in a determined voice.

She grabbed me. No gentle touch, a grab. When I felt her hand on my fly, I hit her straight on the muzzle. This neutralized her for a few seconds.

"You like it that way?" she said. "Do you want to hit me again?"

"No."

"Oy," she whispered, touching her face. "Oy..."

"What?" I screamed. "You said *oy*?"

"I'm sorry," she whispered.

Suddenly I got it. Moscow accent.

"Are you Russian?" I yelled at her.

I ripped the veil from her face. Long blond hair. She collapsed. She was crying.

"Mahmud will kill me."

"Don't worry about that," I said. "Mahmud will not kill you because I will kill Mahmud. I'll castrate him, I'll behead him and drown his corpse in the eternal Nile."

"Don't," she kept crying. "He's my best customer. He is a good man. He just wanted to sell you his Chagall from Alexandria."

"There is no Chagall from Alexandria," I yelled at her. "Marc Chagall painted flying elves, tender lovers lost in beautiful dreams uplifted from the reality below. He painted cute cows, too. This prick Mahmud is flying yellow pigs over a futuristic monstrous city. The technique is shit, the colors are like vomit."

She kept crying. She was obese and blond and about fifty years old.

"You hate Russians," she howled.

"How could I! They gave birth to Bakunin and caviar."

"You hate Russians and you are a pervert, trying to fuck an Arab virgin. Fuck me. Fuck me for free and buy Mahmud's paintings or he will never seek my services again. Then I will have to go with the truck drivers and janitors, if he abandons me." She fell on the sofa, spreading wide her legs, lifting up her long, black dress.

"Mahmud's paintings?"

"Yes," she said. "There is no Chagall from Alexandria. No Picasso. It's all painted by him...by Mahmud."

I gave her ten dollars and two bottles of beer from the mini bar. I asked her to pull down her dress as quickly as possible. Then I tried to calm her, assuring that in fact I do like some Russians, including Shostakovich, Sologub and the above mentioned Bakunin – founding father of Anarchism. No doubt it made her feel much better. I kissed her on the cheek. I told her that she was beautiful, in fact one of the most beautiful women I had ever met, but that she had to go now. I made sure to repeat the word "now" several times. She offered to blow me. I refused. She offered again, as a courtesy. With extreme politeness,

I refused again. I gave her another kiss, this time on the forehead.

She left. I brushed my teeth and watched an Egyptian soap opera, to forget the incident.

5

Dear Reiko. I will go to Luxor and Aswan. Thanks for arranging this work for me. It will be a very welcome change. I will be able to send material in four days. Big kiss to Keiko. I love you. Karel

Dear Karel! Greetings from Keiko. She still thinks you are the funniest person she has ever met. She has this big creature you gave her in Madrid – half hippo, half cat. She calls it Karel-san and she keeps it next to her bed. I guess my daughter really adores you. Well, she thinks you and I are merely two colleagues. Sometimes I feel so embarrassed. I hate lying, especially to a child. As for me, I think about you every day. I am so happy you will do safe work for a few days. I wish I could go to Egypt, to see the Nile, the pyramids. I wish I could listen to the silence of the desert at night. I have never seen such beautiful stars as in Egypt and I have never seen such a beautiful sky. It is raining in Tokyo. Reiko

Even more beautiful is the sky over Johannesburg, I thought, especially when one gets out of the city. But there is otherwise precious little beauty about Johannesburg and she will probably never go there.

Dear Reiko. How much longer must we rely on internet messages? Time is flying, and fast.

Dear Karel. If I were a single girl, I would be with you right now. Maybe. Probably. I really don't know. I like you and I am afraid of you. Can I trust you? Are you real? Are you mine? But I am not single and I am not a girl anymore. I have a daughter and she has a father, who also happens to be my husband. He provides her and me with stability and kindness. He is not a man like you, but there are not many men like you and I am not sure if it is good or bad. He is an honest man. Try to understand. I miss you but I am not alone. I am not free. Reiko

*

"I'll cut off your balls right now."

"Wait," said Mahmud, panicked. He did seem panicked. His forehead was sweating. "I'll kiss your ass. I will even sing Israeli military marching songs."

"Mahmud," I said, "I'm supposed to meet a semi-opposition member of the Egyptian Parliament in one hour. You are spoiling my evening. You are ruining my work. Why did you send me a Russian whore?"

"I'll kiss your ass."

"Do not, please."

"I'll drive you today for only ten Egyptian pounds an hour."

"That sounds better."

Mahmud seemed depressed. He leaned on a dirty table of the coffee house, tears in his eyes.

"You won't buy my paintings, will you? You think I paint shit. I know she told you.... She told you that I painted all of them. You think my work is vomit. You don't like my yellow pigs flying over Alexandria." There was a great dose of self-pity in his voice. "She told me. You prefer cows over Paris. You prefer that Jew Chagall."

"Mahmud..."

"You prefer a killer of Palestinian babies."

"Chagall died ages before the intifada," I howled. "Kiss my ass Mahmud."

"I told you I will..."

"Fuck you."

"All right. That may seal our friendship. I may let you do that. But maybe I should get you someone younger."

"What do you want me to do? Hit the table with my forehead? You win," I said. "I'll buy one of your paintings. I'll buy one if you stop offering yourself to me and if you never send Russian whores my way. I don't sleep with whores. I don't like blondes."

"I swear I'll never offer myself again," said Mahmud. "I'll never send *devochkas* to you. I'll give you a discount on all my paintings."

"Write, 'To Keiko from the Egyptian Chagall,'" I said. "Write it in the corner of the painting. In pink. In Japanese."

"I don't speak Japanese."

"Learn it," I said. "It's time. A new language would do you some good."

6

I first met Reiko in Lima, Peru almost a year ago.

The *Museo de La Nación* in San Borja was nearly empty, a Wednesday afternoon.

A young Japanese woman stood in front of the large replica of Ollantaytambo, the ancient City of Incas. It was summer in Lima, hot and humid, and she was wearing a light cotton dress and simple brown sandals.

I approached her and we exchanged a few words.

She had come to write a story about the survival of cultural pre-colonial traditions in Peru for her magazine in Tokyo. She had come to take photos.

In some sense we were colleagues, and she was alone in Lima. I invited her to dinner in Miraflores.

Later we spoke for several hours and I found out she was married and had a seven-year-old daughter.

I took her to *Rosanautica* on the coast where enormous waves crash against an endless beach. We ate there and watched the waves and the sunset.

All this is a lie. Total nonsense. It did not happen like this because nothing happens like this in my life. But at least it's a nice story of our first encounter.

In reality I made a total ass out of myself, right from the very beginning. Strangely, she didn't mind.

I had been drinking at Curich's place on Bolognesi until five in the morning with two girls, receptionists from the Hotel Las Americas. At two, Tony Curich locked the place and we drank and danced with the women, telling all the nonsense about Mario Vargas Llosa writing his *Story of Mayta* there, at the very table now covered by wine bottles and fresh mussels and shrimp. Curich opened an upright piano and sang *El Jinete* in a heavily intoxicated voice. We all sang old songs from Chile: Valparaiso by Gitano Rodriguez and some forgotten tunes by Violeta Parra. At five we flagged a taxi and sent both girls home, a gallant gesture of real *caballeros,* not demanding anything, even paying their fare. I walked home and by seven I had written an editorial about the political climate in Peru. Then I hung out on the terrace, listening to Shostakovich, drinking strong black coffee, suddenly not feeling any urge to sleep.

At ten I went to the Museo de la Nación, and there she was, "Reiko," looking at some artifacts from the Sipan archeological site.

To say I was speechless would be a huge understatement. I stood there, my lower jaw hanging, no doubt a pre-historic expression on my face. Lack of sleep and a significant consumption of Chilean red a factor. I was unwilling to move, looking at her, while she studied old bones excavated from the burial site.

I did not know if she might be objectively beautiful – to me she was astounding. An elegant skirt, falling straight to her ankles, a dark green blouse, black sandals. I knew she was Japanese from the way she dressed and from her designer bag.

I had to talk with her. I knew I had to do something radical realizing she would soon be done with any dusty bones and then leave the museum as she would eventually leave Lima and Peru. I would have no way of finding her again.

There was not much one could say to a beautiful, well styled, obviously rich Japanese woman, without being introduced. The last thing I wished was to sound desperate, pushy, sleazy, insane, or impolite.

"Good afternoon," I said. In Spanish.

"Good afternoon," she replied in English without smiling.

She moved and I thought I had never seen any other woman walk like that. Her feet barely touched the ground, as if she were levitating.

"Who are you?" I asked. It came out against my will and it did not sound any better than how it might look to read.

"What do you mean?" she asked, stopping.

"I'm sorry," I said. I had been not only stupid but rude. Somehow, I sensed it did not matter. Pushing my luck I told her, "I want to know everything about you."

"Why?"

"I don't know how to explain."

"Try." She smiled. Hers was not a gentle smile. It was the ironic, sarcastic smile of a wealthy woman from an enormous cosmopolitan city. It was a piercing smile, challenging and slightly scornful.

She was not shy. I was sure she had come from Tokyo. After my sleepless night I was not in great condition for wit. I had underestimated her. I had overestimated myself. I probably looked like crap.

"Will you allow me to?"

"Why not?"

She was waiting.

"I wonder whether you would agree to marry me?" I went straight to the point. A very constructive approach, I thought.

She did not seem surprised.

"Thank you for your kind offer," she said. "The only trouble is that I am married and I have a daughter."

Good beginning, I surmised. At least we were communicating.

"That's not really the point," I ventured.

"I see." She smiled.

She looked at me for some time, then came one step closer.

"What is the point, then?"

"The point is: would you ever consider marrying *me*?"

"Who are *you*?"

"A writer," I said.

"Do you write books?"

"Yes."

"What else?"

"Articles."

"Are you a journalist?"

"Yes. To an extent."

"What else do you do?"

"Plenty of things. I watch people. I listen to their stories. I think. I write. I make films. Sometimes, I sleep."

She was still looking at me.

"Do you like Messiaen?"

I was stunned. Why would she brandish a French mystical composer? Olivier Messiaen, I thought: an ornithologist. Did I really like him? I had heard him play in La Trinite in Paris, once. A long time ago. Before he became famous.

"I do," I said. "I like Messiaen."

We confronted one another, silent. The situation was ridiculous and I was incapable of improving it.

"You did not answer my question," I said.

She moved again. This time she came very close to me.

"Why not," she said. "I would. The answer is, yes. But you would have to wait and I cannot say for how long."

We were still standing in the middle of the Sipan Section of the gigantic National Museum alongside the bones of some man – probably an odious bureaucrat or a pathological dictator from that bygone era – who had died hundreds of years ago and had been buried with his precious stones, fabrics, gold.

"Then I will have to wait," I said.

“Thank you,” she replied.

Suddenly she laughed, extending her hand.

“My name is Reiko.”

We were engaged.

7

I called the mobile phone of Sub-Sub Comandante Felipe. The connection was terrible, Todos los Santos some ten thousand miles away. I used my MCI calling card, dialing from a pay phone in old Cairo. It felt ridiculous reaching a guerrilla leader this way but this is how the world was now – even revolutionaries were plugged in to the electronic ether, worked online, were computerized, cell phones in their pockets, memory sticks around their necks.

"*Compañero* Felipe," I screamed.

"Karel, *coño*! Where are you calling from?"

"From Cairo, comandante."

"*Egypto, entonces. De nuestro país fraternal.*"

"*Mas o menos,*" I said.

"We are almost ready," screamed Felipe. "We are going to..."

"Where?"

"Here. In Todos los Santos."

"Ready for what?"

"You know for what! What do you think we are doing here, planting roses?"

"When?"

"Soon *hombre*, soon. As soon as they fuck up again and give us a reason. As soon as we have the moral upper hand."

"I will be there," I said.

I lit a cigarette. A veiled lady looked at me with her big black eyes. Her eyes urged me to get off the phone. The eyes were all I could see of her and these were indeed good looking eyes. Cairo taught me how to be an expert in eyes.

"I'll let you know," said Felipe. "Call again in a few days and I will be able to give you more details. We'll soon take the bridge. And the city. We'll hang their servile mayor and his fat German shepherd on the lampposts and we'll raise the flag and at the end we'll drink to the victory together."

"Brilliant," I said. "Just do me a favor. Don't brag about it too much. I would like to be the only one to cover it."

"Take my word for it," said Felipe. "Only you, baby, only you, old *carajo*."

The veiled woman impatiently paced around the phone booth. As she moved, I caught sight of her shoe. It was quite a regular low heel beaten up shoe, not very elegant. I was not impressed. I had expected more.

"How are chicks in Cairo, *hermano*?"

"Depends. Some are veiled."

"I mean, under that stuff..."

"Some are veiled permanently," I tried to explain.

"You mean they are born with that thing?"

"Seems like it."

"But then...when you are together with them..."

"I'm not together with them."

"Not together with them? You mean, you are alone, without a woman?" he shouted in disbelief.

"Some are virgins," I said. "Others are veiled. Some are whoring for the rich Saudis and other golfers who come here to get laid and to get drunk – to get some juice as they call it. There are some Russians here, too. Do you want me to continue?"

"I'm getting the point. But, there must be some young widows there," screamed Felipe, the leader of one of the few surviving active guerrilla groups in Latin America. "Widows and unhappily married housewives are a blessing for men in the places that are not yet liberated..."

"...by the iron fist of the proletariat," I finished his sentence.

"Correct, *'pañero.*"

"I don't think about that," I said sarcastically. "Not in Cairo."

"You should. I think about it everywhere, wherever false and hypocritical morality and petite bourgeoisie values deprive me of the very basic pleasures of life."

"Touch of the poet, comandante."

I smiled at the veiled woman. I smiled at her eyes – the only available part of her body I was able to smile at. She turned her face away. I was obviously getting on her nerves. She wanted me off the phone.

Sub-Sub Comandante was suddenly in a hurry: "I will see you soon. Call me in ten days but not later. I should know by then. But don't forget to call."

"I will call you in one week."

"We'll use horses," he murmured dreamily. "This time we'll do it the old fashioned way. Frontal attack, none of this modern high-flying nonsense."

We said good-bye to each other and I realized how much I missed Todos los Santos and the insane Sub-Sub Comandante Felipe and his men and women.

I stood there, next to the phone in old Cairo forgetting all about the veiled woman pacing around me in anger. I lit cigarette. I thought about the long hot nights in their camp, the sound of a nearby creek, the taste of guavas and mangos, and the permanent suntan of the faces of local girls. The cheap rum we drank at night straight from the bottle. Cold water from the stream.

Nights around Todos los Santos hummed long and dark, full of the forest. My visits were short. I never stayed more than a few days and they never insisted. There was not much we had in common, though sometimes when the interview was over, the recorder and cameras packed, the notebooks closed, they would ask me questions about far away places and we would talk about Japan and China, about Indonesia and India, about revolution, strategy, defeats. We would discuss Cuba and Western interventions on all continents and they would sometimes lecture me on the conditions under which the people of their land barely survived, or perished.

We drank rum and smoked cheap cigarettes. Once, a girl came to my hammock and we made love but she was a simple woman and her lovemaking was as naive and touching as her dreams. Being with her brought no great pleasure but it was fine, like drinking pure water from the spring and there were no promises and no demands afterwards. The muses of the revolution of Todos los Santos were not my types. I preferred city girls from Japan, Korea, Mexico, Spain, sophisticated and hard to get, capricious, ironic, complicated. Simplicity failed to excite me. Being with the girl was a way of not being alone, and when it was over I asked her to leave. Afterwards I lay on my back, head spinning from cheap alcohol, trying to concentrate on the stars above, on the tall palm trees, feeling the calm of the heavy tropical night.

The veiled lady was still waiting to make a phone call. I apologized and briefly tried to look again into her eyes. She turned her head away immediately. I was overwhelmed with sadness realizing no meaningful communication between us was possible – two humans who consisted of similar flesh, blood, and bone.

Could anything that I might say please her? Could she offer something that would brighten my day? Soon there would be a revolution in one of the most miserable places in Latin America and I would go there to tell the story. In a few minutes, she would return to her house, to a life I knew nothing about. She would never know anything about people like Comandante Felipe, her skin would never be exposed to the gentle breeze and velvet-like water of the sea. She would not taste the rays of sun in a dark eternity of red wine. She did not seem to burn with essential questions about the absurdity of life and the injustice of death. Her life seemed void of passions and doubts. I wanted to say something to her but could think of nothing meaningful.

"Sorry for making you wait," I said, leaving.

8

It was hot and humid. I sat on the terrace of the old Odeon Palace Hotel in the center of Cairo.

I sent reports and transferred images the first night I arrived. Ahead of me was a short assignment for a Japanese magazine and after that, a long flight home, to Lima.

From the terrace on the tenth floor I saw the filthy and dusty roofs of Cairo, and I dreamed about the sea breeze, the gossip pages of *La Repûblica* and the old bookstores of Barranco neighborhood in Lima.

My hotel was surrounded by ugly buildings built in the early fifties. Looking down, one could see thousands of people passing through the narrow streets below. There was nothing unique about this place – the great pyramids of Giza too far away, the Nile River invisible, hiding behind enormous and already dilapidated office towers.

Cairo from the terrace of my hotel looked like most any enormous overcrowded and miserable city. The view could easily have passed for any one of the downtown vistas in Chennai, Dhaka, Guatemala City, or Jakarta: a few tall buildings illuminated by neon lights at night, a downtown with cheap stores and dirty eateries, a sprawl of miserable neighborhoods on one side of the city and a few luxury and often tacky locales on the other, with American chain video stores, American chain restaurants, shopping malls, and Western gas stations with shiny air-conditioned food stores.

In the center, hundreds of thousands of people walked on the pseudo marble sidewalks through dilapidated pedestrian zones – pretend luxury for the working lower middle class. Add in pollution, traffic, peddlers, beggars, offensive noise, repulsive and aggressive music from storefronts, and garbage-covered sidewalks.

Hardly anything remained of a former glory – a few grand palaces, temples, mosques surrounded by irreversible urban decay.

Cairo was still one of the greatest African cities. Its Islamic quarter, riverside, Citadel, its pyramids of Giza were matched only by the labyrinth of narrow streets in Fez and the striking natural beauty of Cape Town. But there seemed nothing comfortable and reassuring about Cairo. One had to board a ship going up the Nile River to escape the dust and regain some calm.

There were moments still when I was happy to be here, such as when Mahmud drove me through the labyrinth of narrow disorganized streets, sharing stories about the Cairo of his youth, introducing me to obscure coffee houses and papyrus workshops, small art galleries and obscure paths leading to the Nile River. But nothing held me here. I was killing time between my work in Gaza and my journey to the south.

Nor did I miss rich cities. I left New York many years ago and reduced my trips to Europe to a bare minimum. There was no particular place on earth where I desired to live. By chance, I lived in anonymity in Lima where not many questions were asked and no allegiance was required. For many years, I had floated with no anchor, moving from place to place, free from all responsibilities except one – to be a witness to the insanity that was swallowing the world – to be a storyteller, to be where essential things were happening. To be myself.

9

Before leaving Cairo, I checked email again and opened a message from an Italian countess, buried in a pile of work-related mails and junk. I had "met" the countess a year earlier on an obscure chat and since then she had kept writing me periodic long e-mails full of foul language and gutter-style offers for an encounter. She was nearly forty-five and still very beautiful – one of those ageless Italian women from the upper class. I had no way of knowing if she were really a countess, but then, what reason would she have to lie?

Dear Karel, I read your articles about Gaza. I enjoyed them but I was not moved – I felt excited. I have been trying to imagine how it feels when a man is in the middle of all that – war, bullets flying around his head, desert dust covering his face. Do you shit your pants, my dear? Does it give you a hard on? I wonder. Do you feel like a prehistoric male? I don't really know what you look like in real life, but I like to imagine you as a big masculine man, an animal with an enormous hose. It excites me and I often masturbate thinking about you.

My life is boring. As you know, my husband died five years ago, I have two lovers, much younger than myself. They are boring, too. They keep whining about the fate of the world. One of them is a Communist, from a very rich family in Milan. He fucks me very hard – so hard it hurts – saying he likes the idea of fucking an aristocratic whore – the enemy. What a hypocrite! The enemy! They are all like this, driving their convertible BMWs, eating in the best restaurants, taking vacations in Mauritius while crying over the fate of children dying of AIDS in bloody Africa. I am not a hypocrite. I don't give a shit about those little bastards in the sub-Saharan wastelands. And the truth is – nobody does. Even you do not. I am sure you enjoy the excitement that your work brings you. You even enjoy your moral superiority over people like myself. But I would bet you are staying in five star hotels with two swimming pools, you have an air-conditioned car with a driver, no matter where you work. You probably spend more money in one day than these poor people you are writing about spend in one year. I understand you. I am envious of you – of the excitement your life is surrounded by. I love the city where I grew up and where I still live – I love Venice. Still, I wish I could be exposed to the brutality of life, to its stench, fluids, and horrible sounds. I wish I could sweat in the arms of a real man. I am so sick of the sissies. I want to be slapped when I say something inappropriate, I want my panties to be ripped off when I am being desired, I want to feel pleasure even if it is connected with pain. Passion hurts. And why shouldn't it?

I would like to experience danger. Don't think I am sick, but I really want to see death. I want to see it with my own eyes, not through the filter of the television screen, not in the comfort of plush seats in an Italian cinema. Take me with you, please. Take me at least once. I will serve you. I will carry your bag, I will pay for everything. At night, you can do anything you wish with me. Just say yes and I will come. Countess

I ordered coffee and answered her email:

Dear Countess. I don't know you. What if you are a monster? What if you have four eyes and five arms. What if one of your ears is missing? I don't like meeting new people. Your letter is disturbing. Are you really ready and willing to travel thousands of miles to see suffering and death? What a morbid type of tourism! On the other hand, why not? Somehow I do understand you. Maybe we can meet. If we do, there will be no strings attached and you will have to do exactly what you promised: you will have to obey me, from the very moment we meet at the airport. I won't have much time to take you around. It means you will have to move. No complaints that your feet hurt, that you have your period, that it's too hot. If you accept these conditions, we can meet. Maybe in one month. I will need to run a story about a guerrilla movement in

Todos los Santos. Have you heard about that place?

Give my regards to your city. Karel

She responded almost immediately:

Dear Karel. I have two eyes and two ears, one nose and one very beautiful mouth. I would send you my photo but I can't do it. What if you would blackmail me?

I accept your conditions. No strings attached. You will not hear one word of complaint from me. And of course, I know about Todos los Santos. I know all about those pricks – bearded imbeciles who are trying to undermine free trade and democracy in their miserable part of the world. I hate all that Commie garbage – that's why I would like to see them with my own eyes. Face to face. As you know, I am free. You tell me when to come and I'll be there. I do nothing in Italy. I run a charity for homeless cats. The cats can wait. Countess

10

I took a night train from Cairo's Central Station to Aswan. The train crossed the Nile and stopped at Giza station, taking in hundreds of foreign tourists with colorful backpacks and appalling walking shoes. I bribed the conductor, securing both beds in a sleeping compartment. After the train moved I was served dinner, then took tea and climbed up with a thin book by Naguib Mahfouz, *The Beggar*.

The train followed the Nile River. I could see little through the dark except illuminated suburban stations flying past the window.

Soon I put the book down, turned off the light and closed my eyes, feeling the smooth motion of the car, listening to the monotonous sound of the wheels. The train sped South, toward the heart of Africa, toward Sudan and the Egyptian Nubian city of Aswan on its one thousand kilometer long journey.

I fell asleep then woke with first light to an almost ancient countryside beyond the window, gray huts and orchards and the river, wide and majestic. Tiny *falukas* and huge ships, a concession to modernity, sailed on the Nile.

I jumped from the upper berth, undressed and washed in a tiny sink, then later called the conductor who brought fresh rolls and coffee. Through the window, I watched the river and thought about a man called Sinuhet immortalized in a book by Mika Waltari. Sinuhet was a doctor of pharaohs, exiled from his homeland thousands of years ago. This region used to be the center of the world. To be exiled from Egypt was akin to excommunication from Paradise. Now the world had changed, and millions of Egyptians were willing to leave this oppressive and poor country, searching for a better life in all corners of the world.

Suddenly I felt profound happiness. I was happy to be back in Africa, to be alive, to be moving along the Nile. I felt very strong, full of energy and ready for just about anything life might offer. I opened the door to the hallway and walked around. In moments like this everything seems possible. Not easy, but at least possible, within reach. I enjoyed the sounds of the wheels, the early morning light, the signs of humble villages, the desert, the river. I was grateful for this moment of simple joy and short break, for the calm before the storm.

*

Aswan was dusty, full of sounds and colors. I traveled by taxi to the "Old Cataract Hotel" where *Death on the Nile* had been filmed. I traipsed for about an hour through the magnificent colonial structure, taking photographs, chatting with the staff, then climbed the hill and found a cafe with all its tables facing the Nile from above. I shot several rolls of film and finally sat down to drink red wine with a hot herbal drink from Sudan. Of all the great views I had seen in my life this was one of the most breathtaking. I could see the old Nile-meter and the island with the Temple of Chum. The River was literally covered with small sailing boats and humble traditional *falukas*. The water was clean, pure and inviting and although flowing through the desert, it looked ice cold from above.

I rented an old Peugeot 504 and asked the driver to take me to the Unfinished Obelisk and to the old cemetery and Nubian Museum, and later to a dusty ancient village, as well as the top of the Soviet built Aswan High Dam. There I rested at the monument to Soviet-Egyptian Friendship and photographed Lake Nasser behind the dam.

I took the boat to Agilika island, to the ancient temple of Philae which had been moved here painstakingly stone by stone, before being covered by water from the completed high dam. I sat for a while on the island pier, drinking ice cold water from a large bottle, talking to a vendor, dreaming about taking a slow boat over Lake Nasser to Sudan or disappearing in the desert for several weeks.

But I had to move on to complete my work, so I soon boarded a train going north –

to Luxor. There, a hotel car drove me past impressively illuminated temples to the Hilton where my room had a terrace facing the Nile.

The dark night felt like silk. I left the hotel and walked along the paved riverside. I sat as close as possible to the surface of the Nile, smoking a cigarette, listening to the calm sounds of the great river passing below. This was Thebes, a place surrounded by thousands of years of history. Roads and buildings changed and people wore different clothes, but the river was the same and so were the sounds of the night, the smells of the desert and the countless stars above. By now the moon was so high that it reflected clearly in the moving water of the Nile and I pointed my camera toward the river but I knew how this photograph would come out – flat and cold, soundless. I lowered my lens in disgust, almost scared. I had nothing to add to this image – I had nothing to add to perfection. All I could do was watch in silence, motionless, humbled.

Luxor felt different than Aswan. It had become a tough, business oriented city, ready to sell its former glory, at a high price. I felt tired after Gaza and Hebron. There was no reason to travel back to Cairo. I negotiated a low priced night charter flight to Paris.

I photographed the Tomb of King Ramses and Tutankhamen. Fighting vicious desert flies I photographed the Temple of Hatshepsut, where a busload of foreigners had been massacred by religious fanatics several years ago. I went to Medinat Habu and the Valley of the Queens and the Tomb of Nephrite.

Before leaving Luxor I stopped at Karnak Temple, transformed at night by the tourist industry into a kitsch display called the "Light and Sound Show." Multicolor laser lights touched the old walls of the great ancient structure and this time I felt no guilt photographing this spectacle. The smells and sounds of the desert and the night were fully suppressed by an aggressively amplified pre-recorded tirade about history. Powerful laser and halogen lights shot in all directions. My cameras could offer only a filtered version of this insanity. I shot five films and then caught a lift to the overcrowded airport of Luxor, full of large charter jets from London, Paris and Dusseldorf.

I drank two cups of coffee and bribed several people from the French charter airline, securing three seats for myself on a tiny Airbus 320.

The airplane took off at 2 a.m. I covered my body and face with two blankets, refusing dinner. I fell asleep as three elderly French tourists behind me discussed the price of papyrus.

11

I landed at Charles de Gaulle at five in the morning. At this hour it felt cold and unfriendly, the coffee shops closed, a few bums hanging around the arrival hall.

I picked up my luggage and took a taxi straight to Montparnasse, to the apartment of my Cambodian friend. She dragged me to the bathtub, scrubbed my back and brewed a pot of fresh coffee. I slept for two hours and when I woke, we made love and ate breakfast together.

The contact sheets looked good. My work in the Middle East and Egypt was over and I was ready to go home. I sent slides to Japan. I wrote to Reiko.

In the afternoon my friend played for me her new piece on a Grand Steinway Piano. It was called *Tribute to the Orange Bean Bun.*

She never spoke much. She hardly went out of her little posh apartment, spending all her energy on composing colorful preludes glorifying various vegetables and fruits of Southeast Asia. Only once she made an exception by writing *Variations on Angkor-Watt Blues.*

She was petite, lovely and extremely lazy. We had known each other for many years. She never traveled.

Now she wanted to talk.

"You know, Karel, for three years now you have been my only lover," she said.

I was stunned. I hardly saw her twice a year. We met only when I had to travel through Paris, not often.

"Is that so?" I wondered.

"You know, it's not easy to find someone," she said. "It takes too much effort. One has to get dressed, travel to a restaurant or cafe, meet dozens of brain-dead people, eat terrible food, listen to outrageous nonsense."

She always spoke dreamily and slowly.

"You can move in if you want to. For a couple of months or forever. You know, I can support you."

"Support me?" I stared at her.

"My father worked for the Cambodian government. My family has stolen so much money that I have no idea how to spend it. And I hardly go out."

"Look, I am not sure if I would like to be supported," I smiled.

"All right. Whatever. I can give you some money. Or you can give me some money. It seems that people lately have no fun in life unless they keep exchanging money."

"Not me," I said.

"Stay," she said.

She was sitting next to an open piano keyboard.

"Why?" I laughed. "Why would you want to live with me? Are you in love with me?"

"In love?" she thought for a while. "Oh, that. Yeah. I don't know. I am so passive and you make me move. You are fun while most people are terribly boring. You don't watch football games and car races. You don't sell things, you don't go to the office every day. You eat Asian food. Maybe I am in love."

She yawned.

"Maybe? Do you ever listen to Schumann or Chopin?" I teased her. "Or to Rachmaninov?"

"Not really," she said. "I've listened to Messiaen, lately."

Olivier Messiaen again, I thought, I'll be damned.

"I went the other day to *Salle Pleyel.* My friend was playing preludes by Chopin. It made me enormously sick. I left. It was monstrously emotional and it felt like he suffered when he wrote it. I thought he was scared and not well and desperate..."

"Exactly," I laughed. "Chopin was in love when he wrote his best music. That's exactly what love is. You defined it very well."

"I see," she said. "Is that really what love is?"

"Sure," I said. "Some people shoot themselves because of it. The greater it is, the less chance that it will end well."

"Was Bach in love?"

"Maybe with God," I said. "And definitely with beer. He drank so much of it that at the end of his life he couldn't reach the keys of his harpsichord because of his stomach."

"Can you ever be serious?" she smiled.

She sighed and touched the keyboard with her long, slender fingers. She played *The Coconut Powder in the Seafood Chowder.* She embraced me before I walked out her door.

I went back to the airport, catching a 1 a.m. Air France direct to Buenos Aires and Santiago de Chile, with a connection to Lima.

12

I left my suitcase unpacked. Brushed my teeth, made myself strong coffee, changed into shorts and a faded polo. I felt happy to be back in Lima, resting on the sofa on the terrace of my flat in Miraflores. The place was high, 10th floor, across the street from a narrow park and the cliff. My flat overlooked the Pacific Ocean, a lighthouse, Costa Verde and Chorillos. I had been in this place, in and out, for almost nine years. I had never lived anywhere else for so long.

For me Lima was as close as it gets to a perfect place. Enormous, cosmopolitan, fucked-up, full of history, different races, full of passion and chaos. It felt like jazz, like blues in a filthy dive at four in the morning. There were all the things I needed – an ocean, nearby mountains, the desert, elegance and filth, beauty and ugliness. Lima's dilapidated center was full of hidden treasures, grand palaces, magnificent balconies, museums, galleries, and "cathedrals" – cheap bars full of strange encounters where indigenous men slept head on table after intensive consumption of pisco and beer.

I had never seriously considering leaving Lima. I had never dreamed about living anywhere else. There was Bali but Bali had changed. There was Tokyo and Bangkok, but I visited these places frequently anyway.

When I first came to Lima in 1992 I knew it was one of the most desperate places on earth. Streets full of potholes, corruption, violence, death, pathetic journalism, sleaze, crime, forged money, gasoline diluted with water, dubious friendships, and commercially oriented love affairs. Those days it was easy to get robbed by eight years old boys with a razor blade between their front teeth. Single women never reported robbery knowing they would risk rape at the police station.

The civil war between the Shining Path and the government claimed tens of thousands of victims, sending millions of poor and scared peasants to the coast. Enormous shantytowns grew all around the city, there in the middle of the desert. Bombs exploded several times per week. There seemed to be no safe place in all Peru. Lima was tortured but still the great capital of a great country.

I stayed in Lima, moving from place to place, finally buying an apartment in the beautiful and green neighborhood of Miraflores, knowing I would have to put up with water shortages, electricity cut-offs, and the various inconveniences of life in a country torn by military conflict. With electricity cut off, I had to walk up to the tenth floor of course. I had to look constantly behind me while walking at night. I had to live with the everpresent feeling of guilt for not being one of those many who were starving just a few miles away, but at least I knew that my money came from work that almost no sane person would dare – covering war zones and desperate areas of conflicts.

With the end of the war, practical life slowly returned to normal, but once in a while I had to dictate my articles over the phone because the local internet system was down and most of the phone lines were in such bad condition that fax transmissions kept failing.

Lima too had changed in the last few years. It used to be the filthiest capital city in Latin America, its collapsing buildings like open wounds, with grass and trees growing from their roofs. Sidewalks covered by garbage, old whores and transvestites working the corners of Plaza San Martin and Avenida Tacna. Even now the city was struggling, but new elegant restaurants were popping up along Comandante Espinar Street, and the imposing mall Larcomar had been carved into the rocks, overlooking the Pacific Ocean. Things had improved, for the rich and for some of the very poor. Now there was a supply of water and electricity in almost every shantytown, and the largest one, Villa El Salvador, had an entire street lined with new stores and eateries. New department stores and shopping malls, fast food joints, video rentals, cafes and bars were growing everywhere, even in the poor parts of the city.

That said, some things never changed. The Central Highway to Huancayo still cut through illegal garbage dumps and prehistoric looking shantytowns built on sandy hills, an ocean of bamboo shacks around the Pan-American Highway. There remained the Lima of Comas and Lurigancho and Canto Grande, the Lima of carton boxes, of sheet metal roofs and bamboo walls, the Lima where millions of children breathed the fine sand of the desert and drank polluted water and worked at the age of ten, sometimes dying before becoming adults.

The revolution had been postponed for now. Indigenous people would have to wait for justice, as they had waited for almost five hundred years. The left wing had been discredited by state propaganda and for the time being ceased to exist as an organized force. No children were named Vladimir or Yuri, anymore. There was confusion though awareness lasted among the poor. They knew who their real enemies were – as they had always known and as they always would.

I felt great attachment to the city, but I could not live there permanently – every two months I had to leave for a long journey abroad. I traveled for work, but also needed to browse through bookstores in New York, Hong Kong, and London. I needed to be in touch with the rest of the world, to see new plays in first-rate theaters, admire new fashions, new designs of shoes worn by women in the world capitals.

It was always a great feeling to know that Lima was here, waiting. My library was here, my bedroom overlooking the ocean, my collection of classical music discs, records and tapes, my friends were here and so were the narrow streets of the charming old neighborhood of Barranco.

There was also an old restaurant on Bolognesi Street, a couple blocks from my place. Its owner played piano and harmonica on Friday and Saturday nights. I often wrote entire chapters of my books there. I wrote most of my letters to Reiko there – the ones written by hand, the ones that really mattered, the ones that I never dared send.

13

Writing was an obligation. It had never been a joy. Since age sixteen I felt it was what I had to do and I never questioned the correctness of my decision.

It did not come easy. To complete a novel I usually had to write two drafts by hand, retype the book on a manual typewriter and finally enter the final draft on computer. Sometimes I cheated, but not much and each book took at least two years to complete.

Journalism and travel gave me good stories, and facilitated encounters with people from all over the world, provided dialogue. Listening to music sometimes helped with the structure of the novel. Other times there was no structure, the story found its own form. I desperately tried to avoid the vulgarity of obvious concepts. I disliked overpowering "grand finales" and melodramatic happy endings. I disliked flirting with death – in real life and in my books, but I could not avoid writing about it, either.

I had never encountered any grace in death. Whenever I witnessed death it was almost without exception violent, unexpected and brutal. None of those who were dying knew what, if anything, would come next. No matter what priests, clerics, and gurus said, they had no idea either. No, these hypocrites who scared their herds to death had mouths full of love. They knew exactly how to cash in on fear of the unknown, building palaces, temples, mosques, and cathedrals upon the horror of dying. Men and women living boring and miserable existences on this planet clung to these hypocrites' words out of fear of what might come next. Religions were more about the injection of anesthesia from the leaders than they were about the opium of the masses. All religions without exception tried to suppress a natural fear of dying, promising a bright continuity afterwards, a continuity that justified the miserable existence of men and women living their empty and boring lives on the planet. While Communists have called religions the "opium of the masses" – and they probably have a point – many scared people long for a drug, the hope that there is something better waiting for them somewhere else. Almost all religions, while speaking about love, are based on fear.

Death was an enormous plunge into the unknown, accompanied by pain and a desire to stay a little longer. At least was what I witnessed, working with death on a monthly basis. Sometimes there was no space for such thoughts – only terrible pain and panic. Death and I became well acquainted in Sri Lanka, Cambodia, East Timor, Bosnia, Indonesia, Turkey – wherever I covered the human desire to kill, destroy, and plunder. I became used to seeing it but tried not to write about it too often in my books. Sometimes there was no way to avoid it.

I witnessed my first death in 1991 in Lima, in Chorillos, where the Shining Path blew up a military truck. I arrived at the scene after three in the morning, tipped by colleagues from the daily *La República*. The scene was one of pure carnage, ten soldiers burned and disfigured inside the truck. One man without a face, still alive. One dying, nothing left from his knees down. We all arrived there before the ambulances and police. Reporters from *La República* got to work immediately – taking photographs of the entire scene, a strong flash of guns attached to their cameras, interviewing those still able to speak.

I had no medical training and could do nothing to help the injured men but felt terribly guilty and out of place. I knew I was not paid to feel guilty and so I lifted the Leica to my face, focusing on the soldier without a face, two meters distant, seeing through the lens the exposed flesh, nerves, and blood, what was left of his head still moving right and left on the sidewalk without sound. I felt nausea and then nothing and then warm and repulsive vomit pouring from my mouth and then the tears that often accompany puking. This was my first time. I would see much worse things later, but this was my first experience with death. I never puked again though it always felt the same – guilt and helplessness. And somewhere deep inside – fear of the unknown.

As a child I had been afraid of darkness and I could not sleep without a light turned on in my bedroom. As a child I had been scared of everything, my imagination painfully vivid.

I was still scared when I was sixteen and I was sick of myself by then, deciding I had to finally become a real man and the way to do it was to plunge into my worst nightmares. I read the books of Andre Malraux and Hemingway and I wanted to be like them, to be able to fight for the freedom of Indo-China, to make love to three Chinese girls during a single night, to be able to describe massacres like the one in Smyrna with elegant detachment and manly compassion, accepting death as the state of things, and to talk about it with women while showing a total lack of fear, with scorn for any danger. Malraux and Hemingway were real men and I admired them, totally ignoring the fact that the former became at the end of his life the Minister of Culture in De Gaulle's government and the latter blew out his brains in absolute desperation, in a drunken stupor and alone. They represented everything I was not but wanted to be. Hemingway never had to look for women – women were always there, no matter how old he became or how big his stomach was. Women were attracted by his masculine aura, by his knowledge of the world, by the sweat on his khaki shirt.

It all went out of fashion in the mid-eighties and started to make a comeback a decade later, but I never cared about the vogue of being a war correspondent and a writer. It was my work and I tried to do it the best I could and soon after I started I forgot about old idols and became obsessed with the roads and towns lost in a jungle, with physical exhaustion after work in the tropics, with new landscapes and stories. There was no way back and I had no desire to go back. Women were always there, many of them, but usually not the ones I cared much about in the morning and it was not much important to be admired by them.

I lost all my old fears after seeing what I was afraid to imagine as a child. I realized there were no monsters living in closets, but I saw men and women with their intestines blown out, disfigured victims, some burned beyond recognition. I did not look at them as nightmares, anymore. They were human beings suffering, in pain. Fear disappeared and what was left was only compassion, the desire to tell the story and to find the roots that had led to their suffering.

What emerged was a new fear of not knowing, of not being able to understand.

While traveling I was soon faced with the discovery that almost every place, every country was different from the stereotype created by Western media.

While writing became an obligation, the search for different, non-stereotypical ways of describing the world became my obsession. Later arrived the natural decision to abandon my roots, to part with the comforting and limiting security of having a strong cultural background, of belonging to a place, a country, a culture or group of people who have a common philosophy and approach to life.

This decision brought an enormous freedom but also a discomforting responsibility. I had to build my own world from scratch, create it with different pieces that belonged to various cultures and philosophies or did not belong to anything at all – only to me.

My books became the result of my lifestyle. They were the purpose and justification. Life would not make sense without writing and there was no way I could write without living this kind of life.

14

After our brief encounter in the National Museum, I took Reiko to Miraflores – to my neighborhood.

I drove her around Lima showing her all there was to see, new and old, great and decaying. I asked her to move into my apartment but she refused at first and it took me two days to convince her to stay in the second bedroom. My apartment was spacious, elegant and, thanks to the maid, very clean.

Our relationship was awkward. Her English was excellent but too academic. She would not play with words, she would not improvise, she hardly made jokes. It was not easy to make her laugh. Our dialogues were often interrupted by long pauses, silences that made both of us feel uncomfortable.

I stopped swearing in both English and Spanish. I warned all my friends she met to do the same. I disconnected my answering machine and asked my friend Carlos to come to dinner with only one woman. Before she moved in I had taken down all the strange underground artwork that used to hang on my walls, replacing it with neutral paintings depicting indigenous Peruvian women with tall black hats and the nostalgic streets of old Hanoi.

While showing almost no emotion, Reiko was obviously interested in everything surrounding my life. She listened attentively when I spoke about Lima, she was charming when surrounded by my friends, she asked questions about my past and plans for the future.

At first she was reluctant to speak about her own life but as the days passed, she opened up and let me enter the fragile world of her memories and dreams.

At night we spent long hours sitting on the terrace, talking about our pasts, about the way we saw the world and preferred to live our lives.

We spoke about Japan and the rest of Asia, about South America, Europe, North America, about arts, philosophy, religion, about everything except what had been said a mere few days earlier in the National Museum. It was a strange week. Her body was next to mine: in a taxi, in my car, on the terrace, in the theatre, but there was no physical contact for the entire week she stayed in my place. I decided not to take any risks. I let it flow. We lived together but were not lovers. We slept under the same roof in two separate bedrooms, washed in separate bathrooms, fell asleep and woke separated by walls.

She was married. It was a marriage of convenience, based on a legal agreement, financial ties, and habit. She had a child. She lived in Tokyo – fifteen thousand kilometers away.

The last night, after she went to sleep I wrote her a very simple letter. I said that I was ready to wait. I said many things I had never said before. I sealed the letter in the envelope and I put it into her bag purse that she had left on the dining table.

I drove her to Jorge Chavez International Airport and we had our last cup of coffee on the second floor of the terminal, overlooking the runway.

I kissed her on the lips and she pressed hers against mine so strongly that it hurt. She left. I waited for her plane to take off and I drove to La Punta in Callao, sat in a small bar overlooking the sea and talked for two hours to an old man about fishing and tides. I had no desire to speak to anyone other than a total stranger. I knew I could not explain what had happened and I did not want to explain.

In two days I received a message from her. She thanked me for my hospitality. There were no promises and no plans for the future.

*

We met in Madrid four months later. She brought her daughter. I flew there to see them. They stayed in one room in a luxury hotel on Castellana, while I checked into the *residencial* by Plaza de Olavide, on *calle* Luchana. I used to write in the bars around there and the barkeep still remembered me. At night, alone, I hit hard on *Carlos Primero* and *cidra*. I was not sure what was going on anymore. I had to write stories about other people, in order to forget my own.

To her daughter Keiko I was introduced as an American reporter, a colleague, simply a good bloke. It seemed she did not suspect anything and in fact there was still nothing to suspect.

At the age of eleven, Keiko had a well-developed sense of humor. She had natural curiosity and we quickly became good friends. She was well behaved, but at the same time very mischievous. At first I tried to bribe her by buying her small gifts and sweets but it was obvious she enjoyed my company even without presents.

Reiko had to work two days in a row and I promised to take her daughter to Plaza de Torros.

"Why is *torero* determined to kill the bull?" she asked after the second fight.

"Because otherwise the bull will kill him."

"But why like this – in front of all the people? Why don't they settle it on a farm?"

"People like to see the fight. They find it beautiful, or at least many of them do. Others come only to see blood and death."

"Do you find it beautiful?"

"Sometimes. I find it beautiful today."

"Why does he let the bull come so close? Why doesn't he kill him right away, if he has to?"

"That would be too easy. It would show that he is a coward. He has to give the bull a chance, he has to let him come very close."

"But what if *torero* lets the bull come too close?"

"Then *torero* dies."

"If so, why is he taking such a risk?"

"Because he wants to impress people who come to see him. And because he wants to prove something to himself."

"Is it worth it?"

"To him it is."

For a while, Keiko stared ahead of her in concentration. Then she turned back to me again.

"Doesn't he feel sorry for the bull?"

"No," I said. "But he loves the bull. He has to love him, otherwise he couldn't fight him like this."

"Can one kill someone that one loves?"

"Yes."

"Could you kill someone that you love?"

"No."

She opened the bottle of water and drank half of it, in a few gulps.

"I think I understand, but I can't find appropriate words to describe it. It's not only about bullfighting, is it? It's about something else. What they see here reminds them about something else, right?"

"Right," I said. "But I can't explain it, either."

Later we went to a small bar nearby, decorated by *azulejos.* Keiko's feet hardly touched the ground as she climbed on the high bar stool and I introduced her to *cidra*, just in a very small glass, to the great amusement of the local crew – hardened and macho bullfight aficionados. She drank her apple wine with a very serious expression on her face while I had mine from an enormous one-liter glass.

After finishing, she wiped her mouth with the paper napkin.

"Karel-san," she said suddenly. "Are you going to marry my mother?"

15

I made myself strong espresso. It was getting cooler outside as I sat on the terrace, unpacking envelopes containing *The Guardian Weekly*, *Le Monde Diplomatique* and *London Review of Books*. I was sorting thick envelopes containing airline upgrades, mileage statements and promotions. There were bills and checks, and only two postcards. These days almost nobody wrote real letters and postcards. I always did, but hardly received any in return.

Green, Chief of the Foreign Section of my magazine, called at five in the afternoon.

"I'm sick of e-mailing," he said. "I want you all in New York on Friday. I'm inviting you, Joanne, Moretti and Hide."

"Fine," I said. "Who pays for the tickets?"

"I will. *The Weekly Globe* will."

"Did I hear you say business class?"

"Fly business, I don't care," he said. "The most important thing is that the four of you arrive. I don't care about the rest. Five of us will have a strategic editorial meeting. We'll have to discuss changes..."

"What kind of changes?" I wondered.

"Many. That's why I have to talk to you in person. I want to hear your ideas."

"Are we going to endorse Republicans?"

"Don't be an asshole," sighed Green. "We're not endorsing anybody. But the world is changing and so should our magazine."

"How is the world changing?" I wondered.

"People are tired of ideology," said Green. "As you would put it, salesmen are running the world. Intellectuals are in internal exile. Everybody wants to be light because the rulers are lightweight."

"Dumb shits?" I tried to understand.

"Karel," said Green. "Why don't we talk about it when you come to New York? Are you really coming?"

"Of course," I said. "Do I have a choice?"

"Please don't put it that way."

"I will be there," I said.

"We'll have our editorial meeting at 2 p.m. at the office. Then I would like us to meet in a neutral place. Just you and me. Maybe we can start at Berry's."

"Fine," I said. "Are you fetching Moretti from Moscow?"

"Yes, you are right, I should. Joanne is coming, too."

I drank my espresso, looking at the waves below. I had no desire to travel to New York. I had just returned from the Middle East. I wanted to be alone with Reiko, in an uncomplicated place, Greece maybe, on some remote island. I felt like swimming, walking on the beach, eating seafood, and olives, drinking white wine, making love until morning, sleeping until afternoon and doing it all over again. I felt like walking along old cobblestone streets of a small and ancient village. I wanted to sit in a local cafe under a big old tree and read and write poetry again and listen to the village folks singing late at night.

"I'll see you on Friday," I said. "I have to go to Todos los Santos in three weeks. We need to discuss that, too."

"Thank you," said Green. "We'll talk. We'll talk the entire night. We'll discuss everything."

16

I came home after lunch, kicked off my shoes, and filled a large glass with ice water. I turned on the computer while watching BBC news. The maid was polishing the wooden furniture with a disgusting colorless rug soaked in a smelly liquid.

I checked e-mail, went through the Reuters cables and decided to have some fun. I accessed Arab Chat, informing everyone in the room that I had recently returned from the West Bank and Gaza Strip.

It worked. I started to receive instant messages.

"What did you write about the *intifada*?"

"Why are Israelis killing Palestinian children?"

"Why is the foreign press so biased?"

"Why are Americans still supporting Israel?"

After a while a short message popped up on my screen: "Hi. I'm Hanan."

"Hi, are you veiled or a virgin? Or both?" I wrote, hoping this obnoxious line would scare her off. I was not in a mood for small talk.

"I'm not veiled," she wrote. "And yes, I'm still a virgin. You?"

"Not really," I wrote. "Not for many years."

"A/l/s?"

"35, Lima, Peru, m," I wrote. "You?"

"25, Amman, Jordan, f."

"How can you be a virgin at the age of 25?" I wondered. I was in an extremely rude state of mind that afternoon.

"God's will," she explained. I checked her bio with photograph. When I enlarged it, I was looking at a young Middle Eastern beauty with big black eyes.

"I saw your photo," I wrote.

"Thank you."

"You are beautiful," I wrote.

"Some people say that I am," she wrote.

"Some people are definitely right. What on earth are you doing? Studying?"

"No, I'm working at the front desk of a large five star hotel in Amman," she wrote.

"And still a virgin?"

"Still a virgin."

"Incredible," I wrote.

"I'm Muslim," she explained.

"Some are Muslims and veiled and single, but not virgins."

"That's true," she admitted, "many are like that. But not me."

"I would never doubt it."

"And you? Are you a Muslim?"

"Not really."

"You are not Jewish, are you?"

"Oh no," I wrote.

"Maybe we can be friends," she wrote. "I read you have just now come back from the Middle East. Do you know my country?"

"Of course. I drove from Amman to the Dead Sea and to Petra and down to Aquaba. All the way to the Saudi border. But that was a few years ago."

"How was your trip?"

"Lonely. Beautiful scenery. Desert. Silence. You know how it is. At night, I felt often alone."

"Why?"

"There is something about the towns in the desert. You can hardly hear anything at night. Not even the wind. And you want to talk, but there is nobody around – the streets are empty. At night you stare at the ceiling and try to remember things from the past and hope for sound, for some voice coming from the distance, for anything."

"Sometimes it comes," she wrote. "Sometimes you can hear a child crying. Or simply the barking of the dogs."

"Yes, sometimes you can. But sometimes there is only silence."

"Maybe I can teach you something about our religion," she wrote.

"Maybe I can teach you about love," I wrote, teasing her.

"Maybe..." she wrote. "But I shouldn't listen to you. How do you look?"

Joke, I thought. It was just a joke. Women all over the world were losing their sense of humor.

"Fine," I wrote. "I look all right."

"No photo?"

"Hanan, I don't chat. I mean I almost never chat."

"Maybe you will convert one day."

"I have no religion to convert from," I wrote.

"No religion? Don't you feel scared?"

"Scared of what?"

"Scared of not belonging to anything."

"No. But I feel scared of belonging to something that teaches people to believe in the unknown."

"I don't understand."

"It doesn't matter," I smiled.

"Ok. It's all right. I like you. Can we be friends?"

"We already are," I wrote.

"I live in a house with my entire family. Too many people around. I have to sign off. I shouldn't chat like this with strangers. Can we talk again, sometime?"

"Sure," I said. I gave her my personal e-mail address and the one at *The Weekly Globe*.

"I wish you sweet dreams," she wrote.

It was 3 p.m. in Lima. Surfers had taken over most of the coast. The sun was still high in the sky.

"Sleep well," I wrote.

"Don't forget me."

"How could I?" I wrote.

"Where did you say you live?"

"Lima, Peru," I wrote. "I am sure you know everything about this city."

She didn't get the irony.

"No, sorry. I don't know anything about Lima. When we talk again, I would like you to tell me all about it."

"It's all right," I wrote. "Next time I'll tell you about Lima. Sweet dreams."

"Thank you. I'll think about you," she wrote before signing off.

A small airplane was flying over the ocean and along the coast. It was pulling a long banner with an advertisement.

Suddenly another message popped up on my computer screen. “You write about us. You should know that in a few days we will be ready to die for Allah. We will kill Jewish dogs and die ourselves.”

“Who are you?”

“We: those who will be happy to die for Palestine.”

“Look,” I wrote. “Take it easy. Why don't you try to live for Palestine, instead?”

“There is nothing that would make us happier than to die for our country and for Allah,” came the prefabricated answer. I had never gotten used to outbursts like that.

“I'm not sure if happiness is the right word,” I wrote.

“You don't understand.”

“I guess I’m not very bright.”

“Jews are dogs.”

“That’s not a very brilliant path to mutual understanding,” I wrote. “There are plenty of Jews in Israel and elsewhere who are supporting your right to have a state.”

“Exceptions don't matter.”

“I believe they do.”

The maid moved into my office, pulling a monstrous vacuum cleaner producing a demonic roar.

“María Elena, por favor.”

Without a word she withdrew.

I went to the kitchen, opened the fridge and poured myself a huge glass of cold Chilean white wine.

"When and where are you going to do it?" I wrote.

There was a long pause.

"Do you think we are stupid? Of course we are not going to tell you."

"Fine," I wrote, annoyed. "I didn't contact you. You contacted me. How do you know that I write about the Middle East, anyway?"

"You wrote that you just came back from our country. We checked your profile and we checked a couple of your articles."

"Fast work. So what do you think about them?"

"You write what you think is right and you are defending our people. You write about our suffering. Thank you. But you are also trying to understand the dogs. You are not one of us. You don't belong to us."

"That's very correct. I don't belong to you. I don't belong anywhere or to anyone."

Another pause. I lit up another cigarette and went on sipping cold fruity white.

"Don't you belong to your country?"

"I don't have a country."

"To your wife?"

"I don't have one."

"To your religion?"

"I have no need for religion."

Another pause.

"We feel sorry for you."

"Don't!" I laughed.

"You must be a very scared man."

"Hell, no."

"You don't believe in God."

"How do you know? And if I don't, why would that make me scared?"

"You play it both ways."

I drank yet another glass of wine. It was tasting better with each gulp.

"Do me and yourself a favor," I wrote. "Before you blow up anything, wait and think it over."

"You can't convince us," came the almost immediate answer. "We've made up our mind. You'll soon hear about us."

"I am not trying to convince you of anything, just asking you to think before you do something irreversible."

"Are you a pacifist?"

"No," I wrote. "I believe that a man has to fight when there is a reason to fight. I just don't think that what you are planning is the correct way to fight. I think one should fight trying to win and not to die in the process. And I also believe that when a man has to fight, he should fight other men, not women and civilians."

Pause.

"We understand your point of view, but we don't agree. When one fights for something sacred, he can use any means."

"Life is sacred," I wrote. "Yours and theirs. If you die, you will never see your land free."

"We will, from above."

"Fine," I wrote. "I don't think we are speaking the same language."

"Good point."

"Therefore we shouldn't waste each other's time."

Pause.

"Wait."

"?"

"You wrote you are in Lima?"

"Yes."

"How is Lima?"

"Warm," I wrote. "Built in the middle of the desert, on the coast of the ocean. The environment is similar to that of Gaza, but there are tall mountains just a few kilometers from the city. It's beautiful, but there was a civil war and plenty of corruption, mismanagement, and poverty. Not all parts of the city are pretty. Some are very depressing, even terrible."

"But you still choose to live there."

"Yes."

"Why not in the United States?"

"I don't know. I used to live in New York. I prefer to live here," I wrote. "Listen.... Let me ask you a question."

"Yes?"

I had another sip of wine.

"Do you really want to die?"

Again, no answer for a couple of minutes.

"No. Not really."

"Don't."

"Look..."

"Yes?"

"We kind of have to."

"You don't," I wrote. "Think about it. I am sure there is a way out of it. I'm sure you don't have to do it."

"We swore. We said we are available."

"And *them*?"

"Them?"

"The people to whom you swore. Are they ready to die?"

"We don't know. We think so."

"You think. But you are not sure. You don't know."

"Look..."

"Yes?"

"Everybody wants to live."

"Live then, damn it!"

"Don't swear. You can imagine it's not easy. But one has to have some responsibility. One has his country to defend. And enemies to fight. We have our religious reasons, too."

"It doesn't have to be you," I wrote. "Does it really have to be you who will explode, who will be torn to pieces? Do you know how it looks, how it must feel? And what if you don't die right away? What if you are ripped to pieces but are still alive? Your brain functioning, your nerves exposed but no mouth to cry out with? No fingers, no legs not even a face?"

"You are trying to scare us."

"I'm trying to tell you what can happen. I saw it happen. I saw it almost every week here in Peru. And elsewhere."

"What were they fighting for there?"

"For right things. For social justice and for indigenous people. But they chose wrong means and they lost."

"We cannot lose. God is on our side."

"But what if there is nothing? What if you do it and there is nothing, absolutely nothing afterwards?"

"There is something. We were told..."

"Those who told you don't know more than you do. Did they tell you what color God is?"

"No..."

"Ask them."

"We'll talk to you later."

"When?"

Pause.

"We'll let you know."

"Fine," I wrote. "Write to me any time you feel like it. You won't do anything in the meantime, will you?"

"No."

"Get some sleep. Think about something nice for a change. Think about some beautiful girl, about the ocean, about a crazy and exciting adventure, about how much fun you can have in life. You never had much fun, did you? But it may change, it may all change one day."

"Thanks, editor."

"Don't mention it. But please, promise me one thing. For once, don't merely repeat, don't believe what others say. Just think. Think before you go somewhere from where there is no return."

I signed off and finished the bottle of wine in couple minutes. It was getting dark outside. I was suddenly scared.

17

I woke up in the middle of the night, sweat covering my body. For a moment I wasn't sure where I was. I turned on the light, relieved to realize I was still in my apartment in Miraflores. I turned the light off again and walked barefoot out to the terrace.

I had a dream about that boy again. I did not know his name. He was hardly fifteen, dark skin, fragile body, long black hair. He came back once in a while to haunt me at night.

He never had a chance against a mob of twenty kids.

I was standing there, in the middle of a dusty road connecting the two small Indonesian villages of Wakal and Hitulama, in the province of Ambon that had suddenly exploded in insane religious violence.

Two cameras hung from my neck and I worked automatically – like a robot: zooming, focusing, shooting.

They were going to get him and there was nothing that could be done to stop them.

The boy ran in my direction, his face perspiring, mouth open, eyes fixed in the distance somewhere behind me. He knew he was going to die. He was screaming something I couldn't understand. He ran toward me, passed me, then disappeared behind my back.

"Stop!" I screamed and they really stopped, machetes in their hands, facing me, grinning at me. My driver had disappeared a long time ago and I was left alone in the middle of the road, facing twenty adolescents determined to kill.

We stood there motionless and then one of them said something I couldn't understand and all of them smiled at me, bypassed me, and ran after their victim.

All over Ambon, Muslims were killing Christians, and Christians were killing Muslims. Churches and mosques were being burned, and there was no end to the spiral of violence which had started suddenly, without warning. Some claimed it had started over an unpaid bus fare. Others blamed the situation on government spies and provocateurs. But the bottom line was that from the very beginning, the predominantly Christian people of Malukas had never desired to be part of Indonesia. Tensions had grown in correspondence with migration from all over the archipelago, sponsored by the government. Formerly colonized, humiliated, and plundered, now Indonesia itself had increasingly begun to resemble a colonial power.

I ran after the group, sweat covering my shirt. I witnessed the moment when they caught up with the boy and my camera recorded the moment when he fell on the ground, being punched and kicked while still trying to protect his face with his hands. I was there when a machete cut his arm right above the elbow and the first stream of blood sprinkled from his veins, I was there when he screamed as sharp blades of knives entered his body, cutting through his pants and shirt, covering everything around him in dark red and then in brown as the blood gradually mixed with earth. And then the boy screamed no more, but they kept cutting into his stiff body, yelling loudly, drunk with murderous joy. When they turned him around, his face was calm and his eyes open. He was dead and I took a few more photographs realizing that the gang was now ready to pose, proud, and satisfied by its deed.

They lifted machetes and knives high in the air, they embraced each other and their victorious roar flew over the jungle. The mouth of the boy was tight shut and his eyes looked straight up, toward the sky.

They came toward me, smiling. One of them spoke some English.

He said: “They are killing our men and women. We're victims here, just protecting ourselves.”

I did not say anything. I did not want to engage in conversation. This was the best moment to interview them, to get quotes. But I felt nausea, I suddenly felt like throwing up, not from the blood but from the look of the faces surrounding me. There was nothing more I wanted to hear from them, so I squeezed the solid metal body of the F-4 camera with one hand, to feel that my brain was still in control of my body.

Eventually they left and I walked slowly up the hill, toward the paved road, where my driver had locked himself in the car, smoking cloves, his hair in disarray, an expression of pure horror on his face. He said he had not expected to see me alive. He wanted to drive immediately back to Ambon City, but I doubled the price and finally he agreed to take me to Hila, a few miles away.

Hila used to be one of my places. I used to go there in order to escape the confusion of the world. It was almost as far as one could travel. Almost no foreigners, hardly any visitors from Java. I used to fly to Ujung Pandang as it used to be called – to Makasar in Sulawesi – and wait for one or two days not even knowing if the small Fokker jet would take me straight to Ambon or leave me stranded in West Papuan Sorong because of bad weather. From the airport there was another one-hour drive to Hila, through the lush green tropical jungle. Hila used to be one of the prettiest small towns in the country, with the oldest Dutch colonial church in all of Indonesia. In its center stood Fort Amsterdam, a small castle overlooking pristine beach, tall palm trees along the coast and clean blue sea. I had come here many times, to write and swim and read books that I had no time to read anywhere else. I had always believed this was one of the last places of sanity in the troubled world, my secret sanctuary.

Now everything lay in ruins. As I expected, the church had been burned to the ground. Nothing was left of it, except a few foundation stones and black ashes. Not one wall had survived.

I found a man, a young curator who used to take care of the church and the fort, and we sat on the shore and I waited for him to tell the story, to recall the plunder he had witnessed, but there was obviously not much he was willing to say. He kept his head low, looking at the pebbles under his feet and there were long and uneasy pauses between each sentence he uttered.

"Today I'm ashamed to be Indonesian. Here, we all used to live together – Christians and Muslims.... We used to intermarry.... There were never any problems here, before. But the human soul has so many dark secrets. Some of them are as deep as the bottom of the sea."

We were smoking clove cigarettes and it was slowly getting dark and I knew it was not safe to stay there any longer, but I had a hard time gathering strength to leave. Another great place had been ruined by religious hatred.

"I'm Christian," said the Curator. "But my wife is from a Muslim family and most of my friends are Muslims. I don't know how I'll be able to look at their eyes and how they'll be able to look at mine. Trust is broken. Once the cycle of violence starts, there is almost nothing that can stop it. I already miss my friends, but I know I have lost them forever. Even if we meet again, we will be holding knives behind our backs."

There were no words of encouragement inside me. I felt empty. We shook hands and I left Hila. As he had lost his friends, I had lost this place forever. From now on I would be coming back to Hila only as a war reporter. There would be no books of poetry, no novels in my bag.

As we drove to Ambon city, I saw young men, machetes in their hands, walking along the road in small groups. They looked determined. I had no idea whether they were Muslims or Christians. I had no idea where they were going and I had doubts that they knew it themselves.

I opened a bottle of Cusqueña beer, still thinking about the Ambonese boy whose death I could not prevent and had witnessed two years ago.

There are some images that never go away, and Ambon in 1999 became an inexhaustible supplier of them.

As I drank beer on the empty terrace, I thought about a girl who couldn't be older than six. She was crying, running for shelter from her burning house that stood next to a church. Both the church and her house were swallowed by flames and she was probably the only one who had survived the fire. She was running away, holding her nose protecting herself from thick smoke. Again, I was merely there, doing nothing to help, unable to help, not knowing how to help, unwilling to get involved. I felt ridiculous, standing there and taking her photograph. She looked very small and very scared and I felt so big next to her. If

I could have made up my mind fast, I could have stopped her, taken her hand, damned my work, taken her to the airport, flown with her to Jakarta, adopted her, hired a babysitter in Lima, let her live in my huge empty apartment in Miraflores, sent her to a good school, taught her English and Spanish. We might have become good friends and all her troubles would have been over and I would at least have somebody to live for, to bring presents to from far away places, to explain things about the world. Instead I woodenly stood there, pressing the shutter, unable to move, too lazy, too scared of the paperwork, of dealing with the Indonesian bureaucracy, of losing my freedom and my comfortably detached way of life. At that moment I knew I was contaminated, too. Fucked up, emotionally subnormal, like all the others I scorned so profoundly. Later on I never got over that moment and I never forgave myself for not stopping, for not adopting that little girl from Ambon running away from the flames of her burning house.

*

I gave images to the world, to men and women sitting comfortably in chairs, lying on sofas, living dull lives. They looked at the photos I took, read my reports, secretly congratulated themselves for being born in much luckier places. They needed my images and they were willing to pay for them. They were willing to pay as long as I made them feel better by showing the agony and misery of others. And I needed their money so I could live my own damned life.

Sometimes all this got to me, so that I woke in the middle of the night, not remembering where I was. I saw the faces of those who had died and of those I had left behind. I felt guilty and I felt responsible for what I had seen and could not stop in Ambon and East Timor, Sri Lanka, Cambodia, Burma, Peru, Colombia, Bosnia, Nicaragua, Chiapas, Todos los Santos, Haiti, Gaza, Turkey, Iraq.

I also knew I could not stop leading this life for as long as I lived. I was free. And scared. And very lonely, sometimes. But there was no going back.

18

"This city is sick. There is nothing sane about it," said Carlos, a painter, my best Peruvian friend.

We were driving to Punta Hermosa, to the beach, on the Pan-American Highway cutting through enormous shantytowns. Fine desert sand covered the edges of the road. I drove my Land Rover at a hundred and forty kilometers per hour, anti-radar on, dark windows hermetically sealed. I hated this stretch of road, I hated the past and present of this country, I indeed hated Lima, yet was unable to live without it.

"Next month I'm going to France," said Carlos. "I'll probably stay there. I'll meet my friends in Paris, go to museums and galleries, drink a few bottles of wine and take a train south, to a little village in Provence. Or maybe I'll go all the way to Italy – to Tuscany. I'll take fifty novels and read them all, read every night until early morning. I'll paint. I'll paint all that I can remember, all that I see there, and I'll cry missing Peru but I'll not come back. I can't work here. Lima is killing me."

I accelerated, passing a bus crammed with people.

“Why not,” I said. “Go if it will help.”

“Exactly,” said Carlos. “Why not. I am afraid we'll all leave, eventually.”

“Maybe,” I said. I did not plan to leave Lima. Not for good, anyway. Not yet.

“I'm sick of complaining,” said Carlos. “I'm sick of whining, of drinking, of fucking almost every night. I'm sick of those big black devoted puppy eyes of women in the morning. I'm sick of their fear of being abandoned, of their horror of getting old alone, I'm sick of having to kick them out of my bed before sunrise. I understand their fear. It's a terrible place to be alone and helpless and poor and old. I fuck almost every night and I bribe officials every day. And I have to breathe this shitty air morning to night, day after day.”

I slowed down. Children from the shantytown were running across the highway.

“Fuck,” I said, pushing the brakes. The car came almost to a halt.

The road cut through the fertile green oasis of Lurin, exposing one side of the great ancient coastal city of Pachacamac, plundered and destroyed in the name of the cross by the Spanish conqueror and notorious mass murderer Francisco Pizzaro. Here, in 1533, he executed all the local priests after failing to find gold. Almost half a millennium later his statues decorate the squares of almost all major cities in Peru while his golden loot covers the roofs and altars of majestic European cathedrals. Catholicism had become the official religion in Peru. Looters and killers were commemorated as heroes.

I sped on the four lane motorway. All around were ugly, dilapidated beach resorts, Playa de las Señoritas, Playa de los Caballeros, blown up tires and garbage decorating both sides of the highway. Peru was fucked up.

We found a little local restaurant on the hill of San Bartolo. Carlos ordered two large portions of ceviche and cold beer.

"You should probably leave," I said. "But I will miss you if you do."

"I will miss you, too," said Carlos. "But you are hardly here, anyway. You say that you live in Lima, but most of the time you are somewhere else."

"I guess it's the only way I can live here," I said.

"You are lucky," he said. "Others don't have this luxury."

The ceviche was fresh and good, with pieces of red potatoes and corn. The beer was ice cold. We ate silently, watching people at other tables: a family on a weekend trip, lovers, an elderly couple.

"Would you be able to paint abroad?" I asked.

"I don't know. I will try."

"Would you be able to find a good substitute for the jungle, its great rivers and ancient *altiplano* villages?"

"I don't know," he said.

We finished our beer and ordered two more bottles.

I thought about Reiko. When she was here, I wanted to take her to *altiplano* but we did not have time. I wanted her to go up with me, all the way – to an altitude of four thousand meters, so I could show her the fragility of the grass and flowers and the humble mud and stone huts that had stood for centuries. I wanted her to see the reminders of a great civilization destroyed by greed and religious insanity. I wanted her to feel the thinness of the air and the extremity of colors. I wanted her to see the faces of the people, wrinkled and dark, motionless. I wanted her to hear their unique music, not salsa – that annoying and aggressive urban jazz from the coast – but *cuecas* and *vaines*, gentle as the color of water in the lakes of *altiplano*, and I wanted her to see how the local girls danced during nights of fiesta, with their cheeks red, black hats on, long colorful scarves flying behind their shoulders, as if there were no tomorrow. Up there one could not readily count on the arrival of a new day. I wanted her to hear the silence at night and the far away whistle of a cargo ship on majestic Lake Titicaca. I had wanted to be alone with her at night, to show her the stars of the Southern sky, incredibly close to earth, as if able to be touched by an outstretched hand. I wanted to show her the Urubamba valley and its river – ice cold and wild, its water rolling over tremendous boulders. But I had not been sure if she would have understood, and I was afraid of rejection, of silence, of the irony – not a rejection of myself but a rejection of this place grown dearer to me than any other on earth. There, ten years ago I had witnessed the birth of a child in a small village next to the city of Ayacucho and I had seen death again and again and I had felt so much hate radiating from the mountain towns I thought it could fill the entire earth. The bitter civil war had divided cities and villages, families and loved ones. Hate ruled, but there was also love, tenderness, so much that I was often left speechless.

"I guess there is always a substitute. For everything," I said.

"As you well know," he said.

We drove toward the bay, parked the car, and walked on the narrow *malecon.*

"I'm sick of so many things, but above all I am sick of desperation," said Carlos. "I'm sick of feeling guilty, and I do feel guilty wherever I go in this country. I can't fight, coño, I'm an artist. I wish I could but I can't. It's different for you. Peru is your country and at the same time it isn't. You are living and publishing all over the world. You spend four months a year in Asia. You don't depend on Peru – you can take off at any moment and move to Mexico or Chile or Bangkok and no one would dare say anything. You have no obligation to this country. You are free."

We smoked, looking at the calm surface of the bay.

"All right," I said. "Let me explain. When I was a child, my grandfather took me for walks through the old city. We always had long conversations. We lived in Prague when it was still gray and ancient, mysterious, almost untouched by the modern age. One evening we arrived at Malá Strana. It seemed the only shining colors were on the roofs of palaces and cathedrals. My grandfather pointed out the roofs and said: 'All that gold and silver has been stolen from people who live in far away places.' He told me about Peru and Bolivia. I was ten years old and I didn't know much about these countries. When we came home I asked him to show me an atlas. We talked almost until midnight. I felt shame. I felt helpless. I felt responsible. Since then I've wanted to come here."

"And you did."

"Yes."

"And you stayed. Why?"

"I don't know," I said.

We drove in silence back to the restaurant.

"Was it because of Ana?"

"Ana is dead."

"Still..."

"No," I said. "She is dead."

"Right," he said. "You wouldn't stay because of the memories."

"No," I said. "I never stay because of the memories."

"I am sorry," he said. "I know you don't like touching this subject."

"I don't."

We entered a humble little restaurant and it was getting dark but we did not feel like going back to Lima.

"Before I leave," said Carlos, "before I go to France, I would like to drive into the mountains. Alone. With no particular plan. I would like to disappear for several days, maybe weeks. I will not miss Lima. I will not miss the noise and music and conversations. I will not miss the traffic jams and decaying streets and buildings. I'll miss the silence of the countryside. And the dirt floors of the Andean houses high in the mountains. I'll miss the smell of eucalyptus, silent gestures, the eyes of the women, all that is never articulated. I dedicated my life to showing what is hidden inside my people. I paint silence. I pain their humiliation and pain. I paint their fear and their dreams and their anger and their hopes. I paint their struggle."

"I understand," I said.

We ordered more beer.

"I feel like getting drunk," he said slowly.

"That's all right," I said.

We asked for a bottle of *pisco* and the owner finally gave us a smile.

"I want us to talk about Ana," he said.

"No, I'd better not," I said.

"I want to. Please. I have to. I want to talk about Ana and about that night."

"Why?"

"Because we never did. Because otherwise I can't leave."

"It happened years ago. Talking about her will not change anything."

He dismissed my words with a sharp gesture of his hand. He didn't look old, but he didn't look young, either. I noticed blue veins in his hands and the white paint stuck at the corner of his nails.

"For me it will. I was involved, too," he said. "You know I was right there when it happened."

"Of course I know."

"We both drove her there and you had no idea what was happening. And then it happened and you still didn't understand..."

He used hands to make his point. I didn't want to pursue this, but I felt like I had no choice.

"Suddenly there was no Ana," I said. "That much I did understand."

"And since then we never spoke about it. Not a single word. Even after we drove back to Miraflores, even after we went to your kitchen and drank all the wine there was in your house, we still didn't speak."

"I didn't know what to say."

"Did you suspect anything before it happened?"

"No," I said feeling unwell.

I emptied my glass and poured more booze.

"That's what I thought. I was sure you didn't know anything. Did you at least suspect she was involved?"

"No. Never. Sometimes, maybe."

"But you drove her there with that bizarre case she held in her lap. Weren't you suspicious?"

"We drove her," I said. "We did, Carlos. It wasn't just me. It was both of us. I thought it was strange but Ana was an adult woman, and, remember, she said she was meeting somebody that night and after we arrived at the bridge, she asked us to leave."

"But we didn't go too far."

I didn't like *pisco* - it almost always tasted of cheap *grappa*. But there was no choice. I called the owner and asked him to put six large bottles of beer in the freezer. For me, cheap beer was always better than cheap hard liquor. At least it was more digestible and less insulting.

“Carlos,” I said. “There is nothing we can do about it now. There was not much we could have done then. She had made up her mind and she was going to do it one way or another. Sooner or later. She made a mistake and it went off before it was supposed to. It's that simple. It was just an error.”

“I don't understand why she was so desperate. She had no reason to...”

“She was not desperate. She decided to do it and she didn't do it well or the equipment failed. She definitely didn’t want to die.”

“But she knew she could...”

“She did, I suppose,” I said.

“Do you think she was a member?”

“Probably.”

“Are you sure you didn't suspect anything?”

“I'm sure,” I said.

“She lived with you.”

“We never spoke about these things.”

“Fuck,” he said. “I never got over it.”

“I try not to think about it,” I said. “Sometimes it comes back and I wonder what could have been done. Probably nothing.”

The night was dark and the air cooler than in the city. By now, almost everyone had left San Bartolo. We had been hearing dogs barking in the village. Otherwise, there was silence. The real absolute desert silence.

“So you have no regrets,” he concluded.

“It's not about regrets,” I said.

He lit up his cigarette and looked somewhere behind my back.

“Ana was the only woman I loved in my entire life,” he said. The way he said it, it sounded somehow detached, as if he were describing a painting or event that had occurred a long time ago, to someone else. "If you would not have appeared, I would have asked her to be my wife. Everything would have been different. I knew she was involved but I never told you. There was no reason to tell you. I would have convinced her to leave, to escape, to run away with me. To have a family, children, a normal life."

"To run where?" I asked.

"Wherever. Far away. To Brazil, to Europe, to Mexico, somewhere."

"What about your work?"

"My work," he smiled bitterly. "What would matter? Nothing, except her, mattered."

And I knew it was true. That was what he felt. 'Damn,' I thought.

"I'm sorry," I said. "I didn't know. I understand now."

"Of course you didn't know. I made sure you didn't."

"I thought you two were only friends."

"That, too. And much more than that."

I had no idea what to say.

"It's fucked up," I said. That was true. That much I knew.

"It is," he admitted.

We had another drink. I was slowly getting used to cheap *pisco*.

"She never meant anything to you," he said. "Did she?"

"Not much," I admitted. "Not as much as she meant to you, I suppose. Or at least I thought she didn't mean much to me. Before it happened. Then things changed. She became very important afterwards."

"Too late, don't you think?"

"Too late," I admitted. "Does it make any sense to you?"

"What?"

"All this," I said.

"You mean about Ana?"

"Yes. And no. Everything."

"I see." He lit up another Hamilton, finished yet another shot of *pisco* and chased it with a glass of ice cold beer. "I don't know. I guess you have to make sense out of it, somehow. Or blow out your brains or start the revolution or do what Ana did."

"Right," I said.

"I'm sorry," he said. "I'm sorry I insisted on talking about Ana."

"I'm glad we did," I said. "It's fine now."

We drank in silence and I kept looking at his face. He was probably my age, thirty-five, maybe bit older, and his skin was dark and his eyes almost oriental. Once again I noticed his veins and then the stains of colors he had been mixing when I picked him up at his studio in Barranco.

"I would like to photograph you," I said. "Before you go to France."

"Don't bother," he said. "It's a waste of your time and film."

"I would still like to do it," I insisted. "And I would also like to apologize. I didn't know anything about you and Ana. If I would have known, I would have let her go. Probably, almost definitely. But I didn't know and you didn't find the courage to tell me and everything got fucked up and I feel terribly sorry now. And it maybe doesn't matter anymore, but I want you to know how much I regret what happened."

"Thank you," he said. "It does matter. It matters a lot."

We drank.

"Have you ever loved a woman?" he asked, suddenly.

"Why? Of course I have."

"Have you ever loved a woman so much that you never wanted to be separated from her. That you wanted to share absolutely everything that you have and what is inside you with her?"

"I don't think so," I said. "I think we are always alone, no matter what."

For a while, we were again surrounded by the silence, both thinking our own thoughts.

"I still don't understand what you are doing here," he changed the subject. "Why are you really here? Why in Lima? Is Peru really the best place on earth for you?"

"No," I said. "Probably not."

"Then why?"

"The mist," I tried. "The mist and the sand coming almost to the shore of the Pacific Ocean. The small old houses and streets of Barranco and Miraflores. The women – the way they walk, the way they smile and the way they love. The small film club in Barranco. The anarchy of life. My friends. My memories. Curich and his piano recitals on Saturday nights. The omnipresent Andes and the jungle immediately behind them. The merciless silver waves of the Pacific Ocean. The used bookstores. Cafe Haiti next to Kennedy Park. The editorials by Mirko Lauer in *La República.* La Punta of Callao. The brutality and tenderness, all mixed together. The greatness and the decay. Do I have to go on?"

Carlos was concentrating on the foam of his beer.

"Maybe," he said. "But it is also a place where the majority of people live in misery. Where children have to work, and some have to prostitute themselves. It's a place where doctors extract human organs from their patients and sell them to the rich countries. A place where you can't go to the center of the city at night. Where every ruler is a thief. It's one of the most segregated places on earth. This is my Peru. Now which Peru is real, yours or mine?"

"Both," I said. "Fuck, Carlos, you know it. Both countries are real."

"I'm going," he mumbled. "I'm going away. Lima is a rhapsody in gray. I miss the brainless green lush colors of continental Europe. I would like to meet a girl somewhere in Italy. Simple and kind. She doesn't have to be beautiful, but she has to be very simple and gentle. I want her to worry about the mortgage, I want her to think about money and ask me how much I sell my paintings for. I don't want her to ask me what is hidden behind my colors, I don't need these long conversations about misery and pain, mysticism, suffering and death. Do you understand? I just want to wake up in the morning and smell fresh coffee from the kitchen and see stuffed animals on the floor of her bedroom and I want to see her naked body and her smile and I want to know that over there, behind the window nothing happens, nothing terrible, just ordinary life, and orange designer public buses are taking ordinary people to work, and men and women are drinking cappuccino in bars with little marble tables and the girl that I will meet – I want her to talk on the phone to her girlfriends for hours about nothing as only simple women do, and I want her to wear beautiful shoes and I want her to dance with me at night and speak straight, without doublespeak, I want her to be ignorant about my past, about my country, about this goddamned continent that is as dear to me as my life, but a life that despite everything I want to forget and leave behind and I don't know if I ever could, I want her to kiss me good night truly believing that the night will be good and quiet and silent and the next morning the same as the previous one, simple and bright, and I will marry that girl, the girl I'll meet in Italy and we'll have many children together, and we'll laugh together..."

"Carlos," I said, concerned. I felt like shaking him, waking him up.

He was staring down at the plastic cover of the table and I suddenly had a terrible intuition, but it went away and I leaned over the table and embraced him, but he kept staring down and I said: "It's all right, it's all right, *coño*." And it came back, the intuition. I felt something would happen, something terrible might happen soon, but I did not know what it would be or what to do or how to prevent it and I let him go and sat back again and poured more *pisco* in my glass and chased it with cold beer, this time straight from the bottle.

Suddenly, Carlos lifted his eyes and looked straight at my face: "One week after she met you, Ana and I drank coffee at Haiti in Miraflores. She said, 'I don't know if I'm in love with him, but I am sure I am in love with the lightness that he brings to my life.' Do you remember how you were? You used to drive north to Tumbes with her and you would both swim and play in the water for hours. You were joking every minute, you made her laugh, you made us all laugh, all the time. You were writing funny poems and satires in your terrible Spanish, you danced with her without knowing how to dance. You have changed. It got you, too. Lima. It got us all."

"The war did," I said. "The war here and the war everywhere I covered it. The desperation got me. Not Lima. I came here as a kid and I grew up here and became a man. That simple. Many things happened, not all of them pretty."

"You don't realize it," he said. "Your skin has become thicker, you have become like us almost, no scruples, no regrets. I wanted to be your best friend since we first met. For the same reason Ana wanted to be your woman. There was no heaviness around you. No cynicism. You were free, but you have changed."

"I'm afraid it's the contrary. Freedom is heavy," I said. "There is only lightness in belonging to something or to someone. And I don't know if I still know how to belong."

We left the place a few minutes before midnight. I drove slowly north on the *Pan-Americana*, toward Lima. The night was cool and I turned off the air-conditioner, put down the windows and opened the sun roof. The sky was covered by thousands of bright stars – proof that we were still far from the city – no smog, no pollution.

Radio Mar played old boleros. Carlos took off his shoes, and stuck his feet out the window. We drank beer straight from bottles purchased at the restaurant in San Bartolo, breaking empty ones against the asphalt of the highway.

"Do you know what keeps people in the slums going?" he asked suddenly.

"What?" I stared at the black asphalt ahead of me.

"They think that God is Peruvian."

19

I read through several work-related emails. My journey to New York had been arranged. My latest book was ready to go to print in London.

There were other new emails, those from my relatives and friends, and of course, one from the countess.

Dear Karel. I keep thinking about my upcoming trip to Todos los Santos. I imagine brutal, smelly men in green uniforms and terrorist masks, how they unzip their flies before penetrating a woman. If you would only know how tired I am of Italian kids and their Armani jackets, how bored I am with the marble tables of cafes. I am dead bored with yuppies and businessmen, their obsession with sports and car races. One of them invited me to join him at a Monza Formula One race. He got me a ticket. I slapped his face and I said: "Little bastard, you want to impress me – get into that shit yourself and drive it. Or get yourself a Range Rover and take me for a ride in Bhutan." I was also invited to a football game one of those days. Can you imagine: me at the stadium surrounded by brutes smelling of beer? I hate them all, soft asses, little dicks, cowards. I went to the opera last night and fell asleep during the second act. It never happened to me before. I feel almost suicidal – boredom is killing me. European Union effeminate men will soon turn me into a lesbian. Save me. Take me to the jungle. Beat me up. Rape me. Sodomize me. Do anything. Just make me feel alive. Countess

Dear Karel. I received the photographs you took in the mountains of Peru. I felt so happy. Beauty, finally. I wish I could be there with you. Sometimes I feel concerned about your obsession with wars and human suffering. I know, I understand that you find beauty even in the most repulsive moments and in the most desperate places on earth. We are so different. I long for harmony and for beauty. The lenses of my cameras always search for that perfect moment. Your photos often accuse, they are offensive, insulting, scary. Why? I know you as a happy and cheerful man. When I am with you, I cannot stop laughing. But your work is monstrous. Of course it's great, of course I admire you – but still it's monstrous. There must be so many things that I still don't know about you.

I would like to be with you, right now. But how can it be arranged? Do we even have the right to be together? Can we build our happiness on the misery of someone else? Think about it. I miss you and I wish I could be with you. I wish I knew what to do. Reiko

Dear Karel. I can talk to you openly because I don't know you. We have never met and probably we never will. Let me make a little confession here. And believe me, these words don't come easy to a conservative Arab girl like me. I'm 25 years old. I have never even kissed a man. More and more I feel my virginity and total lack of physical love as a burden. I pray. Every day. Well, almost every day.... But lying on the bed alone at night I feel so restless. My body is longing for something. I know I have no right to ask you this but I will: Can we talk about it? Can you answer some questions I need to ask? It has to be you – a foreigner. I would never dare speak about these things with an Arab man. Not even with my girlfriends. These topics are taboo in my country. Can we chat, please? Let me know when you are available. I need to talk about these things with someone who is not part of my culture – with someone who is open. With someone who will not judge me. Yours, Hanan

Editor. We were thinking about you. We think you are a good man, despite the fact that you can't fully understand us. Maybe you are a Jew, but even that doesn't matter. Life here is so hopeless. The end of the occupation is nowhere in sight. And we have our internal problems, too. Sometimes we watch foreign films and we feel a bit envious. It would be nice to go dancing and surfing, to have girlfriends, to be carefree.... But our girls are mostly covered and they cannot go out with us, freely. All of us are very poor. And we have a religion that is very strict and obliges us to live in a certain way. We have to obey our parents who live right next to us, in the same overcrowded dwellings. Sometimes it feels that we never really had a childhood, sometimes it feels that there is not much we can lose.

We'll soon have to do what we swore we will do, editor. It's our obligation. We are not happy about it, but our love for this Country and for God is stronger than our fear and our desire to live. Or at least this is what we have been taught to feel all these years. You'll hear from us. Your Palestinian friends

Karel, you whore! We work for the same motherfucking magazine but we hardly see each other. I'm coming to New York and so are you. Brilliant! Green is falling apart, he is scared – he has a news phobia and he is afraid of everything, especially of us.

Moscow, as you know, is ridiculous, snobbish, nationalistic, poor, oligarchic, prostituted, ugly, restless, pretentious – simply wonderful. Putin is restoring an empire. He is doing it slowly and secretly. But Russia is finished, no matter what he does. It has been finished for more than 80 years, now, maybe more.

What is Green afraid of really? What is this "strategic editorial meeting" all about? Is he going to fire us all? He thinks that we are falling apart while we all know that he is the one who is.... He is concerned. He knows "something is happening," but he doesn't know exactly what. The end of democracy? The end of globalization? The possible end of the universal dictatorship of capital? A new war? A new era? Is the Third World going to unite? Is Hugo Chavez a new prophet? Let him guess. Let him be scared. We won't tell him. We won't tell him mainly because we don't know, but he'll not guess it. He'll get drunk and he'll beg us for clues. When he called me, he complained that you and Joanne had entered a disturbing and strange realm of surrealistic uncertainty – you ask too many questions in your articles, and our readers seem to be unable to answer them. Green drinks too much. He goes out with older women. He's too fat. He is only fifty five but he looks well over the hill. He reads Umberto Eco and Coelho.

I am looking forward to meeting you in New York. Your friend, Gino Moretti

Karel562, join the Korean wife-swapping e-group. Post pictures of nude Korean wife or girlfriend.

Bankruptcy? No problem, we can help.

20

Two nights before Reiko's departure from Madrid, I sat in Cafe Arco Iris working on my fifth double *Carlos Primero,* reading Dostoyevsky's *Notes From the Underground,* when Reiko showed up. It was close to midnight and I was taken aback when she walked in. I had grown weary of being her tour guide to *Reina Sofia* and *El Prado* and to all the places where Hemingway dined and drank himself silly, and to El Escorial and Toledo. I needed to be alone and work out the concept of my new book.

She came straight to my table, sat down and ordered lemon soda with ice, no alcohol.

"Karel, I love you," she said. Just like that, no prelude, no hello, no small talk.

All that followed that night was simple.

I paid the bill and we went to my *residencial* and we made love for the first time, twice without speaking, and it was much more than I would have ever dared to expect. Later she took a shower and we made love again, very slowly and I tried to speak to her body with mine, begging it for understanding and permanency and then we opened the window and it was just the two of us in the entire city.

In the middle of the night, Madrid was unusually quiet and there was an ancient church right across the street and Reiko was lying naked on white sheets, holding a *Nobel* between her slender fingers, blue smoke sailing out into the night through the window.

"Does it mean anything to you?" she asked.

I took her into my arms and again I tried to tell her without words that yes, that it meant a lot, that it meant everything, that she was all that mattered and the rest be damned forever. We both felt exhausted but could not sleep and there was still so much we wanted to confess, so much we wanted to learn about each other. Our silent dialogue went on till the morning, until the first sunlight entered our room and we finally fell asleep for the first time together. I had a dream about her being here with me in one of those very rare and unique moments when reality and dreams merge and become one.

21

There was really nothing we could agree on. Chasing her perfect images, Reiko traveled the world over; two Leicas neatly packed in her small equipment bag, searching for early cherry blossoms, new UNESCO World Heritage Sites, opera houses, important museums and galleries. Meanwhile, I was stuck in filthy military barracks close to the frontline or grilling some corrupt president or prime minister. Reiko was engaged in elegant conversations at cocktail parties arranged by elites. She was voluntarily ignorant of politics, of misery, of the unjust arrangement of the world. She believed that beauty could resolve all problems of humankind.

When we met in Spain, she drank champagne or very chilled white wine. Her hands and feet were elegantly groomed. Her shoes, blouses and skirts fit perfectly. She never raised her voice, never fought, never swore.

Reiko adored romantic dinners, dim lights, chamber music and candles. I liked smoky, noisy establishments with cigarette butts covering the floor, *tapas*, cheap house red and *cidra*, old bars filled with loud crowds where harsh and cheeky Castilian jokes flew through the thick cigarette smoke.

Later when the lights in our hotel rooms were dimmed, she changed and became a very simple woman, open and passionate and a little insecure. At night we tried not to discuss anything in particular but sometimes we exchanged stories from the past, waiting for desire to return, waiting for the morning light to appear through the windows, our clothes on the floor in total disorder.

Once I brought some old poems of mine and I read them to her at night. I used to write and publish poetry, a long time ago. Now the poems were stored in a file in Lima, squeezed between thick volumes of *The History of the United States* by Andre Maurois and *The History of the Soviet Union* by Luis Aragon.

Time. I felt it run at an accelerating pace. A year used to be an eternity. Now it was just that – a year. 365 days spent in Peru and Indonesia, China and Cambodia, Venezuela, London, New York. Marked by the impersonality of hotel rooms, airports, restaurants, full of new and mostly insignificant encounters, kitschy native music shows, Oriental and Western operas, my time now was marked by women whose names I could not remember a month later, by the piles of books I read on the go.

Reiko was not afraid of time. She knew she would age beautifully. She knew she would live until ninety as her grandparents had. She had no profound doubts – she belonged easily to her own culture. Her passion for life was natural, physical. Her passion had no part of desperation, no revolt against the present or the past or against the pace of time. She never cried after reaching an orgasm. Ana used to cry. Once she slapped my face, hit my chest with her small fists. She used to penetrate my skin with her long nails. Ana used to cry at night when she thought I was asleep. She was afraid of time. As much as I was. Probably more.

After our first lovemaking I missed Reiko and the great simplicity and beauty of the nights I spent with her.

After returning to Peru I put several photographs she took on the living room wall. All were perfect and I liked to be surrounded by their sublime perspective in Lima. One depicted a gentle morning mist over the Chinese city of Suzhou. Another caught the bright smile of a street vendor of mangos in Calcutta. I put a print of a narrow alley in Nara at night on the wall of my bedroom. Reiko provided negatives and I blew them up big and hung them on the walls without frames. These photographs showed an integral part of Reiko, a part I still did not know well.

When my friends in Lima asked who took these photographs, I did not know what to answer. Sometimes I would simply say "a great Japanese photographer," or "a lady I know well. My friend." There were more honest answers but I would never give them: "The wife of somebody else. A woman I am in love with. A girl I occasionally have sex with. A mother of a child who is not mine."

We wrote to each other almost every day. It was not enough but it had to do for now.

The next day I was leaving for New York and she had to fly to Kuala Lumpur and then Bali. Reiko was documenting a story about foreign painters who had settled down in the old village of Ubud.

I lit my cigarette, looking down at the dark mass of the Pacific Ocean, that tremendous mass of water separating my world from hers.

22

George W. Bush was about to be sworn in as the new president of the United States of America. He was expected to give a speech to all citizens, rich and poor, white and black, stupid and smart, fucked up and happy. He was going to give his speech to me, too. I increased the volume though a US military fanatic howled aggressive medleys of patriotic songs into his microphone. It all looked very embarrassing and I lowered my eyes, almost blushing. The election stolen, black and poor voters excluded from casting ballots, the nation with no real choice.

There was a car bomb explosion in Tel Aviv. Two Palestinians had died – blown themselves up – and there was no way of identifying their bodies. One elderly woman had died too, twenty Israeli civilians injured. I checked my e-mail: there was no message from the Middle East. I refused to make a connection. I lied to myself: they will write tomorrow, or maybe several days from now.

An instant message from Hanan popped onto the screen.

"Hi," she wrote.

"How are you?"

"About the conversation we had.... And about the e-mail I wrote to you..."

"Yes?"

"You are not angry, are you?"

"Of course not."

"I would like to ask you something..."

"But of course."

"It's very indecent."

"I think I can handle it."

"I don't want you to think that I am a bad girl."

"I'm sure you are not."

"You promised you'll give me some advice."

"Advice about?"

"About..."

"Yes?"

"About.... well..."

"What do you want to know?"

"You know I am still a virgin."

"Yes. You told me."

"I have to stay a virgin until I get married. Because of my culture. More precisely, because I was told that I have to. I never question what I am told, we are not supposed to do that here. Another reason I have to remain a virgin is because nobody would want to marry me otherwise."

"Right," I wrote. "I know what you are talking about."

"Do you think that something happens if I.... I feel so embarrassed to say it."

"Don't be," I wrote.

"Do you think that I would lose my virginity if I tried to..."

"To do what?"

"You know, that thing that one does alone..."

"You mean, masturbating?"

"I guess that's what people call it," she wrote and I felt her blushing ten thousand miles away. "I feel so terribly..."

"Why would you feel terribly?" I wondered. "Hanan, darling, everybody in this world masturbates." I looked at the television screen. "Even my president does, although it probably looks very peculiar. There is no reason to feel bad about it."

"I never did," she wrote. "I just read about it. Sometimes I read forbidden things online. But that's a secret."

The power of the internet, I thought.

"Never?"

"Never."

"Well..."

"I want to know if I would lose my virginity if I did it."

"Of course not. But again, it depends how you do it."

There was a pause.

"That's exactly what I don't know..."

"Just don't put anything inside, you know..."

"Can you teach me? Please..."

"Me?!"

"Yes. Please. Can you teach me how to do it and remain a virgin?"

I went straight to the kitchen. I dragged out a full bottle of Sauvignon Blanc, uncorked it and had some, right from the bottle. I went quickly through my entire sexual past. It unzipped itself into my brain.

It was colorful but was I really qualified to help a pure Jordanian virgin with the act of masturbation?

"All right," I wrote.

"Thank you very much. You are so kind. I felt that I could count on you. Can we start?"

With the Clintons about to leave the Presidency, despite the pathetic and disappointing results of their administration, I felt sad because their disgrace was proof that even the most educated and intelligent people could not change the system anymore, could not change the order – the world dictatorship of elite market vendors. What would come after the Clintons seemed monstrous, but in many ways it would not change the general course.

A couple of years after Bill Clinton had been elected President, I drove to Hope, Arkansas where he had been raised. I spoke to many people who remembered him when he was a young. He was poor and grew up with children of other races. He definitely knew what was going on in America; he did not have the excuse of not knowing. I always believed that he had entered politics thinking he could bring positive changes but that later, when confronted with the system, he backed off and became a conformist, and I think far worse than that. There was Plan Colombia and the Somali adventure. There was much more. Under his leadership all hope for a progressive Democratic Party disappeared, and all hope for leftwing Labor and Social Democrats vanished across the Atlantic.

A few years ago I wished he would resign and make a statement that the system is corrupt and works against ordinary Americans. It was naive on my part. After all, he had shown himself to be a typical political animal, caring more about his position than about the country.

"Are you alone?" I asked Hanan.

"Yes. My family is visiting relatives outside of Amman. I have locked the door. They are coming back in four hours."

"All right. Are you dressed?"

"Yes. I am wearing a skirt and blouse. And all that a woman wears underneath."

"You'll have to.... Ok. Relax. Is there some boy you like?"

"You," she wrote.

"No. Look, seriously, somebody you know well."

"I am serious. I found your picture in the magazine you write for. Can it be you?"

This was getting personal. Ridiculous. Touchy. Touching. It was the first time for her and I had to make sure it would not leave a bitter aftertaste. I mobilized some leftovers of my sensitivity.

"Think about being kissed gently on your lips. Caress your neck with your fingers. Slowly. Don't rush."

"Yes," she wrote. "I think about you kissing me."

"Unbutton your blouse."

"Yes."

"Slowly."

"Yes."

"Touch your breast through your bra. Use both hands. Find your nipples."

There was a pause.

"Are your nipples hard?"

"Yes."

"Good," I wrote. "Think about someone kissing them. Caressing the top of them with the tip of his tongue. Then slowly going around them, pressing the tongue deep into your breasts."

"President Clinton, distinguished guests and my fellow citizens, the peaceful transfer of authority is rare in history, yet common in our country. With a simple oath, we affirm old traditions and make new beginnings. As I begin, I thank President Clinton for his service to our Nation. And I thank Vice President Gore for a contest conducted with spirit and ending with grace...."

Disgrace, I thought. The democratically elected President Gore was being thanked for not fighting, for not defending the will of American voters.

Pause.

"Feels good."

"Pull up your bra. Play with your breasts and do it very slowly and gently."

"Yes."

Long pause.

"Now take off your skirt and panties."

Pause.

"I did."

I felt like I was landing a 747 jet in very turbulent weather and with zero visibility. Her orgasm was the goal, the end of a runway. But I was still a few hundred feet above the ground and had to bring the plane straight over the navigation beacons, without distraction, without losing the course, not too fast and not to slow. At least she had her landing gear down and I had begun to extend her flaps.

Of course I had only a blurry idea of how women masturbate. My experience had been limited strictly to a few occasions when they had *insisted* on showing me. But it had just been a part of a game. This was for real.

I disconnected the autopilot and went on manual, using my imagination.

"Spread you legs and caress your stomach."

There were some tactics that never failed. Like sucking on a woman's knees or massaging her inner thighs with a very strong thrust of tongue. But it was done by a man. Hanan was not an acrobat and I had to make the entire process as simple as possible.

"And now touch your inner thighs."

"Yes."

"Whatever you do, think that somebody else is doing it to you."

"Yes."

"And take your time. Don't rush."

"Yes."

Long pause.

"Is it wet?"

"Sorry?"

"You know..."

"There?"

"Yes."

Pause.

"Oh my god, yes. Very."

All right. The runway had appeared. It was still far away, but at least it was visible.

Then the phone connected to the second line rang and I answered.

"Karel? This is Green."

"Hi Green."

"Do you see it?"

"No. Oh, you mean that... Right. Yes."

"Are you with a woman? Should I call later?"

"No, it's all right."

"What a speech. Do you hear it? *We have a place, all of us, in a long story – a story we continue, but whose end we will not see.* Can you write an editorial, Karel? Just one optimistic one? Please. With some hope in it?"

"You mean you want me to endorse Bush?"

"Not to endorse. Just write something positive about our future foreign policy..."

"Now find your clitoris," I wrote.

"Sorry?"

"The clitoris..."

"What is it?"

"It's that little thing. Above your...you know. Above that thing that is wet right now. It's covered by skin and is very sensitive. The little thing, there..."

"Oh that. Yes."

"I can't do that, Green. Ask somebody else. You know what I think about him and about the whole thing."

"I knew it," said Green. "Are you all on strike? Joanne sent me to hell. Moretti laughed at me. I am afraid to call the others. Do you all hate Republicans?"

"It's not that," I said. "It's not hate, Green... It's worse than that... I simply cannot do it."

"Now wet your fingers and caress your clitoris. Whatever way it feels good. With one finger only, or with two..."

"What if I put it as an ultimatum?"

"Then I would have to resign."

"Just like that?"

"Just like that. I have no choice."

"All right, forget it. It's not an ultimatum."

"Oh God, it feels so good," she wrote. "I am thinking about you. Can I think that you are doing it to me with your tongue?"

"You are coming tomorrow, right?"

"Yes, I will be there," I said.

"Of course you can. Now move faster. Think about something beautiful. Think that someone is now inside you. But don't put your fingers inside. Not deep inside. Otherwise you can damage..."

"I understand."

"Have a safe flight."

"Thanks."

"*We will build our defenses beyond challenge, lest weakness invite challenge.*"

"This is... I never felt like this..."

"Do it faster. Caress your nipples with your other hand."

"Yes."

"*We will confront weapons of mass destruction, so that a new century is spared new horrors.*"

I'm sure you will, bastard, I thought. But not your own and those are the only ones that have brought any horrors to anyone so far.

She didn't type anything for a while.

"The enemies of liberty and our country should make no mistake: America remains engaged in the world by history and by choice, shaping a balance of power that favors freedom. We will defend our allies and our interests..."

At least on this account he was honest, giving us all a taste of what lay ahead.

"Are you all right?" I wrote.

"Oh my god. Something happened. I'm so scared..."

"What happened?"

"When I did what you said... I suddenly felt so strange. I felt weak and then it came, like some wave and I screamed. I can't explain. I screamed so loudly and then I felt weak and defenseless and soft..."

"You had an orgasm."

"Sorry?"

"An orgasm," I wrote. "It's what happens. It's why many people choose to have sex. To feel this – what you described."

"Is it normal?"

"Of course it's normal," I wrote. "It's more than normal. It's one of the greatest things in life."

"It is..."

"Did it feel good?"

"Yes. But I didn't expect it. And now I feel so tired and lonely. I don't feel like doing anything else. I don't feel like thinking. I just want to hold you and I want you to say something to me."

"Why don't you rest now..."

"I will. Karel, but I feel it again... I think I need to do it again, right now. Can I do it again?"

"Sure."

"Will you allow me to?"

"Don't ask me. You can do anything you wish. But remember, don't put anything too deep inside, not even your fingers." I sounded like a Jewish mom.

"I understand that. Thank you. But I mean, is it normal that I want to do it again?"

"It's absolutely normal."

"Thank you. I think I can do it for an entire day."

"Why not?" I smiled at the screen. "There are much worse ways to spend the day."

"I love you," she wrote.

"Big kiss going your way," I wrote.

I had managed to land it, now I had to press on the breaks. All the way, down to the floor, and crawl out of the cabin through the emergency exit.

"This work continues. This story goes on. And an angel still rides in the whirlwind and directs this storm. God bless you all, and God bless America."

This was one of those rare moments when I wished there really was a God, so that he would appear suddenly in front of the television cameras and say something very, very pointed, straight to the face of George. That he would bless him with one great kick in the ass. That would truly be such a blessing to America and to the whole world. But God did not appear. The faces of George's supporters and those of their collaborators remained serious and their words went unchallenged.

"Will you ever talk to me again? I feel so terribly close to you, after what happened. Please."

"Of course I will talk to you again," I wrote.

"If you would be a Muslim, you could take me as your second wife. I would rather be your second wife than the first wife of someone my family will eventually force me to marry."

"I am not married at all," I wrote.

"Really? But are you thinking about converting?"

"Converting?"

"To my religion."

"I have nothing to convert from," I wrote, smiling.

"I should teach you about my faith."

"That would be very kind of you," I wrote. "Now rest and don't think much about anything..."

"I will talk to you soon again. Thank you for everything, my beloved."

There was a loud military salute and the TV cameras showed thousands of people watching the ceremony. Some were crying. Crowds of people were always waiting for something – in Washington, in Russia and Germany, in Italy, in China, in the Vatican and Mecca, in football stadiums and rock concerts. These supporters of whatever came in the thousands, in the millions to express their allegiance to just about anything or anybody who offered them a simplistic option, an easy way out of responsibility. The people of crowds needed to feel that they belong to something greater, that no one is alone, that there is no need to make complex decisions. The people of crowds needed security. Later, they never accepted responsibility for any horrors. Even when millions of innocent people were slaughtered in the name of their religion or their state, they felt innocent. They had merely happened to be there, cheering and shedding tears, wearing the same clothes, waving like banners, thinking bumper sticker thoughts.

Dear Karel, I keep turning to you in my thoughts. To us. Separation is brutal, isn't it? It's all my fault, but you have to understand. We have to be patient. Reiko

Karel, you whore! How are you? I'm pissed drunk here in Moscow, hoping I'll be able to make a flight to New York. Do you believe that whore was finally sworn in? Now he's going to put that honorary white Republican chick into his administration and we'll have a second cold war in no time. The Russians are pissed off no end. Of course from the very beginning these elections looked like the ones in sub-Saharan Africa. We all know that it really doesn't matter which whore makes it to the White House. They don't govern even over their own farts, anymore. Out of control power is now firmly in charge, wrapping itself in ridiculous populist slogans like 'freedom,' 'liberty' and 'democracy.' Damn it – freedom for whom? For the fittest? Didn't that whore

Mario Vargas Llosa call the Mexican PRI 'a perfect dictatorship'? What would he then call the entire world – the new world order and market fundamentalism? Is Green going to fire us all? Is it going to be our last supper? Is he going to try to relocate us? I'm not moving from Moscow. Be damned if I will. Gino Moretti

I put the unfinished bottle of wine back into the refrigerator, corked it, prepared strong espresso and went to work on the editorial about the future foreign policy of the United States. I wrote for three hours, saying all that I wanted to say – all but guaranteeing that it would never go to print. That night I could not care less.

I was starting to suspect that if things continued this way, I would eventually lose my marbles. Something had to change. I had to slow down. There was no stability in my life. It had been fine until now, but suddenly I knew I could not go on like this anymore. I felt as if I were sailing on a ship that had no rope to tie itself to a port. My ship did not even have an anchor.

My plane was leaving in a few hours. I collapsed onto the bed fully dressed and fell asleep almost immediately.

23

The world was full of stories that nobody wanted to print. Some were minor, some were of much greater significance. More than half of the countries I visited were ruined, impoverished, disease-ridden, indebted, seemingly beyond salvation. There was no point in writing about them – demand in the "developed world" was too small, and unless there was an outbreak of civil war, epidemic, or famine – no major magazine or newspaper was willing to dedicate much space to the daily grievances and horrors of poor peasants in Sudan and Bangladesh or indigenous people in Bolivia and Guatemala.

The UN and others published statistics, defined poverty lines, set rules for what could be considered extreme misery. I had never understood these statistics. According to my observations, the great majority of people in the world lived in despicable conditions. I never calculated their purchasing power but I listened to their stories and I saw their dwellings, their streets and the places where they had to work.

Most of the poor countries in the past had been brutally plundered by colonial powers.

Some continued to be plundered. Independence often meant very little – historical borders had been erased. Popularly elected progressive governments had been bribed, undermined, or overthrown outright. Local elites continued to serve foreign masters, and militaries almost everywhere in the poor world were willing to enact bloody coups as long as they were guaranteed a sizeable portion of the loot. Corrupt regimes – mostly sponsored by the West – were offered loans which disappeared into the pockets of the few, while the impoverished majority was expected to pay the bill. The poorer the country, the more likely it would yield to the demands of transnational companies and to the geopolitical interests of the rich countries.

While the developed world headed toward secularism, the more miserable countries increasingly pushed toward conservative forms of religions. The poorer and the less educated the people – the greater became their religious zeal. The misery in the world was too hard to take, apparently. The prospects for the future too bleak. The imaginative brilliance of life after death was often the only hope poor men and women held. But religion also reduced their zeal to fight for a better world during their lifetimes. It taught them obedience. And the West – busy destroying progressive secular governments all over the world – covertly continued to support a lot of the most extreme religious factions, so long as the religions helped guarantee that the majority remained submissive.

Capitalism had outgrown any overall usefulness. It had stayed in charge for too long. In the past it may have been necessary. It may have even been progressive, in its own time. Now it had exploded into an uncontrollable global force, undermining all basic democratic institutions even in the rich countries themselves. Its only justification had become an argument that almost all other attempts to create a more just and humane world always collapsed due to the greed, incompetence, and longing for power of rulers who originally promised to bring a better life to their people. No matter that many of these attempts were marked by interventions from the rich world, by embargos, military actions, and outright terror conducted in the name of freedom and democracy but which in reality served only one purpose: the preservation of the status quo.

To write about these issues in the mainstream media had become almost unthinkable. One could publish books on the topic but even that meant risking being sidelined and expelled from the comfortable life of the officially recognized and tolerated intellectual elite. The punishment for dissent was relatively harsh: being placed outside the system. Being a rebel guaranteed nothing in return, and that has been true even since long before the time when powerful publishing houses and bookstores became mindless business ventures, undergoing mergers aimed only at commercial success. Market fundamentalism buried independent and progressive thought far below the mainstream.

I tried to keep my balance between two worlds, unable to forward to my readers the outright lies offered by the establishment, while too comfortable with my cars and posh apartment, too scared to become a real outcast, to become poor. Unwilling to be an intellectual prostitute, I was not yet ready to become a martyr.

PART II

24

Reiko woke late. The sun was already high in the sky, hiding somewhere behind the heavy snow clouds. Keiko had left for school several hours earlier. The house was quiet.

There seemed to be no reason to get out of bed yet. Tuesdays were slow. Reiko would attend an editorial meeting at two o'clock, then pick up slide films, batteries, notebooks, and guidebooks for her Indonesian trip. She would leave for Bali that night.

Her husband had left for work at seven. He always left the house quietly, at the same hour, five days a week. Never earlier, never later, unless he was traveling. He always made up his side of the bed, neatly. He never woke Reiko in the morning. They had been living together for almost twelve years and every day he followed the same ritual. At night – at ten thirty sharp – he took a bath, dressed in pajamas, and by ten forty-five entered the bedroom, parked his slippers under the wide Western bed and set his alarm clock. Every once in a while he made love to her, silently and without much creativity. Sometimes he turned on the television, falling asleep shortly after. The television was equipped with a timer – it switched the set off automatically at midnight.

There was nothing bad or sinister about him. He was a decent man, only five years older, reasonably attractive, well dressed and groomed, very successful and rich. Hard working, the manager of a large advertising company. He was modest and quiet. Exactly the type of man lonely women would describe in personal ads when looking for a "serious relationship."

Their family life was routine and lacking for nothing, ostensibly. There was sex, or at least twice a month there was sex. There was stability, a substantial dose of it. Money and security, politeness and tolerance. And trust. There was a child – Keiko. Once a year the whole family took a trip to Hawaii or Europe, visited theaters and museums, went to opera. Sometimes there was tenderness, not much of it, but some.

In theory there was nothing wrong with their marriage. Reiko's husband never lost his temper and almost never went out drinking with his colleagues. He never insulted her, never screamed at her, never hit her.

Perfect marriage, she thought.

But now she had a lover.

She moved her feet from under the comforter. She knew her feet were beautiful, well groomed, elegant. Her husband never paid any attention to her feet. He took her feet, as he took her entire body, for granted. When he made love to her, the lights were off and her body was hidden in darkness. Karel, her lover, kissed her toes and her feet when they were together, which she liked because this was where she was sensitive.

Her lover was the opposite of her husband. There was nothing stable about him. She was not sure what his identity was, what his goals in life were, to what class he belonged. There was nothing conventional about him. He brought uncertainty to her life with his love and his words, with the images he created, with insanity and passion and outbursts, with his poems and books and stories. And he said he wanted her more than anything else in his life.

She had never been in love before and she was not sure she had the right to be now, but something had changed – now her life seemed different. She was desired, aware of her body, more sensitive than before but scared and confused. Her life before him was dull. He taught her extremes – desire and fear, loneliness and longing, uncertainty and physical joy.

She did not know what to expect of the future. She still did not know how to read her own dreams which had become abstract, with no concrete shape, leading to no particular outcome.

Reiko left her bedroom and took a shower, letting hot water caress her body. She got dressed quickly and turned on her computer. There was a message from him. It was unusually simple.

She thought for a while, then hit reply.

Dear Karel. Have a nice trip to New York. I am leaving for KL and Bali tomorrow. You can phone me. I will be staying at Four Seasons in Ubud. I'm sure you know the place. I wish you could be with me and show me the island. I will be thinking about you. Love, Reiko

She reread the message and it felt cold. Still she sent it and then sat in front of the computer for several minutes. She suddenly felt the need to say something more substantial and she typed quickly, without thinking about consequences.

Karel. Today I woke up very late. It is cold in Tokyo. The roofs and sidewalks are covered by snow. I am shivering just looking from my window. And not only because of the weather. I feel lonely. I don't know if this is right to feel and to say (after all I'm a married woman). I guess it is wrong but I will say it anyway. I love you. I am afraid I am in love with you. I've never written these words before. Please don't take advantage of my weakness. She erased "weakness," replacing it with "feelings." Then she continued writing. *Don't leave me. But don't push me to act. I still don't understand what is happening. I don't know how to act, what decision to make. I don't want to hurt you, but I don't want to hurt anybody. I will think about you in Bali. I will think about us. I want you and I am afraid of you. Reiko*

She sent the second message, waited for confirmation and turned off the computer.

As Reiko rode the train to work, she opened his book that she had bought the previous night in one of the Roppongi bookstores, the only one of his books translated into Japanese. Although, she had no difficulty reading English, she had picked this one. The book started with these words:

It was not in the morning, it was late at night when two men in gray suits arrived at his home. He was not surprised. He did not even wonder what the purpose of their visit was as he asked them to sit down. He was scared and not certain what to do and what to say – whether to offer them a cup of coffee or water or a glass of wine, or whether to try to leave, to escape using the back door. This was Chile – not Prague, not the imaginary and abstract world of Kafka's "K" – and he knew there was no place to escape nor to hide, not now, not anymore, and so he asked the visitors in the gray suits to sit down with a cup of coffee that they refused to accept.

"Are you…?"

"Yes!" he said, without waiting for whatever they might say. "Am I under arrest?"

It took them some time to answer. "No. Not really. Not yet, anyway."

"Then..."

"We came to talk," said one of them. The taller one. The thinner one. The one with the flashy tie.

Reiko arrived at her station. She closed the book, left the train, and walked toward a tall and modern building within which the office of her magazine occupied the 32nd floor. Her heels played a soft melody on the marble sidewalk. An older man stopped, and followed her with his eyes.

She had written a letter. She had never written those words before. A short letter but she knew he would find it significant.

"K," she thought, Kafka. Chile. It was so far away. So different. She had understood the words she had read, but did not know how to relate to them. She knew Kafka only as a great Jewish writer she had been made to read but had never managed to understand. And Chile for her was desert in the north and the tremendous frozen fjords of the Fire Land in the south. Plus volcanoes, lakes, orchids, high mountains, and the endless coast of the Pacific Ocean. She had never paid much attention to Chile's past. Yes, a coup on September 11th, 1973. The military took power. Long years later, they were voted out. Karel had lived in Chile. He had worked there for awhile. He loved the country, but with a bitter desperation that she had never managed to understand. It was all irrelevant now. Right now she felt like buying a new pair of shoes that he would like. She felt like buying a bunch of flowers. It took her some time to make up her mind but once her mind was made up, everything seemed simple or at least possible. She felt like dancing, like doing something frivolous and light. Instead she pressed the button inside the elevator and felt the force of gravity as the elevator moved her up in silence.

25

The beggar working the corner of Broome and Spring Street looked mean and moderately dangerous. He seemed like a cliché of a beggar, a stereotype. Dirty and slightly bent down, smiling but not friendly, tall and skinny, bullying but not directly aggressive.

"Hey mister, got a quarter?" The same old tune.

I kept walking.

"Hey mister, I'm talkin' to you."

Right, of course. I kept walking.

"Fuck you!" I heard behind my back.

My brisk answer: "Fuck you, too, and your mother and sister and your entire family..." this only in my mind, of course.

I kept walking toward Berry's, where I was supposed to meet Green for a discussion of the failure of the extraordinary strategic editorial meeting held at two that afternoon. This time it was supposed to be "just the two of us so the record can be put straight."

At eight in the evening this traditional bar was still empty. Well over forty years old, a fairly well-preserved post-yuppie woman sat on the bar stool, exposing her well cut calves in dark stockings and expensive looking low heel shoes. She was smoking, constantly checking her watch. She had been drinking Stoli with cranberry juice on the rocks – a mix definitely out of vogue since the Reagan years. I seated myself at the bar, far away from her, ordering pastis on the rocks with water on the side so I could mix it myself.

"Hi," she said almost immediately, moving closer to me. "How are you? My name is Cathy."

"Hi Cathy, I'm Karel," I said.

"Nice meeting you. Are you waiting for your girlfriend?" I could not help but think that this had an early eighties kind of stench. In many ways New York remained outrageously old-fashioned.

"In fact I'm not."

"Oh," she seemed to be more encouraged. "Are you alone?"

"I'm waiting for my friend," I tried to be informative, relatively friendly, or at least not too rude.

"That's nice," she reassured me. "I'm here alone tonight."

"There are times when it's great to be alone."

That sounded melodramatic, pathetic, and I knew it. I did not feel like talking with her. I wanted her to leave me in peace. She seemed to think there should not be times like that.

"I had a hard day at work. And felt like a couple of drinks."

Great, I thought, damn, as she moved even closer to me, to the stool right next to mine. I downed my Pernod and asked the barkeep for another and then changed my mind, took pity on her, asking instead for a double Stoli straight and a regular Stoli with cranberry juice on the rocks for the lady.

Green entered almost immediately after our drinks arrived. He was wearing a dark, funereal looking suit and a yellow power tie with blue squares. Green was an impressive looking man – tall and fat. It was cold in New York but he was sweating.

"Am I late?" he barked.

"It doesn't matter," I said.

He gave me a big hug, all but crushing my bones with his enormous bear-size paws.

"Who's that whore?" he whispered in my ear.

"Cathy," I whispered back. "Cathy," I said loudly introducing her to Green. "And this is Green, Chief Editor of *The Weekly Globe.*"

"Nice meeting you, lady," said Green, opting for politeness, after some hesitation.

"Well, do you have a first name?" smiled Cathy, obviously impressed and interested, checking him out from head to toe.

"He does," I replied instead. "But it's of no importance. He is simply Green. That's what everyone calls him."

Green thought this was funny. He started to laugh and it was too loud and slightly out of place. Cathy did not seem to mind. She was obviously used to corporate schmucks and Green was more tolerable than most of them.

We left Cathy at the bar and moved to a small round table, Green ordering a double single malt, while I stuck to the double Stoli with no ice, straight.

"The strategic editorial meeting was a failure," started Green, taking off his cashmere coat, throwing it onto the next chair, breathing heavily. "I know it, you know it, there is no secret that we were not able to understand each other. We were not even able to communicate intelligibly."

I lit my cigarette, waiting. Smoking was out of date, too, but I didn't care. I was a New Yorker, an exiled New Yorker. That came with some privileges.

"I invited the best of you. Moretti came, you came, Joanne, Keensley, Hide. You all traveled here and I am grateful. You even agreed to talk to me," he said with a dose of sarcasm, and then he paused, sipping his drink. "The only thing is that I understood almost nothing about what you were saying. It is obvious that the foreign section of *The Weekly Globe* is falling apart. I've thought about replacing you, all of you. I've thought about relocating you. The only problem is that I know I can't get anybody better. Maybe things are too complicated and the problem is not you."

"Well..."

"Well what?"

"Where is the problem?"

"I don't know," Green sounded defeated.

"Are sales down?" I asked.

"No. It's just...I smell a disaster. I smell shit – a problem heading our way."

"Why do you think there *is* a problem? Why do you think the foreign section is falling apart?"

"I'm not sure about anything," sighed Green. "Something strange is going on. Something I don't seem to understand. A few years ago, things ran fairly well. The magazine received legible, intelligent reports from its field offices. All of you were clear and concrete. Things were in control. Under my control. Under the control of reason. Then something happened. Your reports became.... What's the word?"

"Abstract?"

"That's exactly it. Thank you! They have become abstract."

"When?"

"Are you asking me?" He finished his drink. "I don't remember exactly when, but it was a gradual process. Now things are definitely confused. Almost all of you now ignore the basic fact that our magazine is not a literary or philosophical club. It's supposed to inform. It's supposed to inform people who haven't got the slightest idea about what's going on in this world and who really don't give a shit about it. They read articles about foreign countries because that was what they saw their fathers do and also because they don't want to look like total assholes. They definitely don't read them in order to complicate their lives or, God forbid, in order to think. They don't want to become intellectuals. They want to be left alone, gently reassured that their uncomplicated vision of the world is correct. Eventually they want to learn one or two smart phrases so they can impress their boss, their wife or secretary."

"Go ahead," I said. He was surprisingly making some sense.

Green wiped sweat off his forehead. He ordered more booze.

"Look, I myself don't particularly like what I'm saying, but somebody has to be honest or we'll all lose our jobs or run *The Weekly Globe* into the ground. It would be a pity, it's becoming one of New York's institutions. So let me put it this way: you all have lost contact with your readers. You have forgotten who your readers are. You are not writing for *Le Monde Diplomatique*. Your readers have never heard of the *New Left Review*. You are writing for a large American magazine that provides middle class men and women with information. Many of these people are simple folks, Forrest Gumps, and you may be tempted to call them uneducated pricks, but every week they pay $4.95 per issue, and thanks to them we are all getting our fat salaries, plane tickets, and per diems. But – if you keep writing your abstract works of art, your useless masterpieces, they will finally turn to the Sports Section of some tabloid and we will all be fucked. They will read the Help Wanted section, instead. They will study horoscopes. You'll not educate them, it's too late for them, you'll just lose them altogether. They don't understand what you are talking about. You know that most people in this country don't like intellectuals. Intellectuals have beards and some of them burn flags.

They don't watch the same films as other people do. They have friends who are fags and women's rights activists. Many intellectuals don't even like sports and their women refuse to watch soaps in the afternoon. They don't go to church. They are outsiders. They are snobs. They have different accents and some of them even speak French. Many of them weren't born in this country. American people don't like snobs and they don't like intellectuals, damn it."

Green was sweating, getting excited, messed up. Cathy sat at the bar, her legs crossed. She looked in our direction. I smiled at her, to relax the atmosphere, and she let one of her shoes slide from her heel to dangle from her toes. Good move, I thought. A pity that Green had lost all interest in the surrounding world. He ordered more drinks. He was getting into it. Analyzing and drinking.

"I respect your opinions. That's why I invited you all here. And I'm going to meet you, one by one, and I am not going to let you go before you explain to me what is really happening."

"I don't know more than what you do," I said.

"You do know more," said Green. "Something is happening. Something scary. Something that justifies your total indifference to our readers. Something I still don't understand."

"Things have become more complex," I tried.

"I am not an asshole," Green informed me. "I know that the situation is confusing. We don't have many enemies, anymore. We have mostly friends. Friends that don't like us. Friends we cannot trust. We have Saudi friends, for instance – that's extremely confusing. Simple Joe doesn't like many of our friends, either. He despises the French and Japanese, partly because he knows that the French and Japanese despise him – simple Joe. He thinks it takes five Poles to screw in a light bulb, but Poland is now in NATO. Many Americans look down at Latinos, they are afraid of Asians, and absolutely refuse to note the existence of Africa. They think that Saudis ride camels and put bed sheets over the heads of their women. Moretti tried to explain everything in one of his editorials. From Moscow. Eventually he just hit the bottle. He is falling apart from all that friendship. Our Moscow office is turning into a bordello, our Russian secretaries becoming single mothers. Moretti hired two new typists he doesn't need, from his own salary. He has his 'zapois,' whatever that means. Still, he manages to write well. The only problem is that nobody wants to read his dispatches."

"You didn't tell him any of this today," I said.

"And what the hell should I tell him? That he writes well, maybe too well for this magazine?"

Green was getting drunk. Not pissed drunk, but drunk all right.

"Look," he said. "I hate this place. It feels like we are in London or Toronto. I feel like they'll kick us out before 11 p.m. I have a car parked outside. Let's get out of here. Let's go to a real place. Let's go to a bar where we can find normal people. Somewhere in Queens or in Brooklyn."

"Aren't we going to take a plane there?" I asked.

"Again! Snobbism. Scorn for the simple reader. Don't you want to see him – your flesh and blood reader? People who come here read *The Economist* and the *New York Review of Books*. Let's see a real American man, a hard working prick who pays for the booze that we are now drinking."

"All right," I said. "Let's see him."

"Or her," added Green, suddenly being politically correct.

There was no escape.

"And let's take the whore."

"Whore?"

"What's her face?" he pointed his fat and large, sausage-like finger toward the relatively well preserved woman in her forties.

"Her name is Cathy," I reminded him.

"Let's take Cathy," he said. "I bet she is at least a Deputy District Attorney, anyway. Let's go."

"How did you know?" She had obviously overheard part of our conversation. "I work for the DA's office."

"Professionalism," said Green. "Let's go."

"Where?" she asked with evident hope in her voice. Her feet in black stockings were slipped well inside her shoes again. She quickly gathered her belongings, left the tip on the bar and approached Green.

"We are driving to a low class pub in Williamsburg," explained Green. "We are going to search for our readers so this young writer can rediscover America after a long leave of absence."

"Why don't we stay in Soho?" she wondered. "Or why don't we go to the East Village? Williamsburg is getting posh, anyway."

"No," said Green. "We have to go to someplace where a hard working American man sits down at an obscure drinking establishment in order to calm his sorrows, quench his thirst, and share his simple vision of the world with his friends after a long day of intensive labor."

"Sounds like a Soviet poster from the 1930's," I muttered.

"Maybe I shouldn't," sighed Cathy.

"You definitely shouldn't," I advised.

"But you will," said Green, triumphantly.

26

We crossed Manhattan Bridge and drove through several blocks of a depressing area of warehouses until we hit one of the decently lit neighborhoods of newly-posh Williamsburg.

There it was, waiting for us on one of the side streets: a macho Polish blue collar bar lit-up by an old fashioned blue neon light. Inside, a large photograph of the son-of-a-Bush hung surrounded by bottles of hard liquor, a photo of his father hung right next to him. Ronald Reagan, the Pope, and Lech Walesa decorating the other walls, together with faded tourist posters of Krakow and the Black Madonna from Czestochowa. Crossed Polish and American flags stuck out from an empty flower pot.

Draft beer of extremely dubious quality was served in enormous plastic cups called "canisters." Old hits by Bruce Springsteen blew from the shiny jukebox while several members of the right wing proletariat consumed a toxic looking liquid from small glasses.

"I grew up in places like this," said Green, tears in his eyes. "These are our people. Our readers, simple folks..."

"Soil of the nation," I added between my teeth.

"Baboons," whispered Cathy, scared.

The owner of the place did not like us from the beginning. He did not like the silver Saab we parked in front of the bar. He could not stand Cathy's elegant outfit, and he did not like the way Green and I were drunk simply because we were drunk in a different way than the other patrons of the bar. He did not bother to hide his aversion, but to his credit, at first he tried to be professional and reasonably civil while dealing with us. He immediately filled two canisters with beer.

"Stoli with cranberry juice," ordered Cathy.

"No Soviet shit here, lady. Wyborowa. Polish," he barked.

"Wyborowa, Polish. With cranberry juice," blushed Cathy. "On the rocks, please."

"Jim Bean. Triple. Two," ordered Green.

Damn, I thought. We drank.

"Well," said Green. "Now you will tell me."

"There is nothing to tell."

"There is. What is *possessing* all of you? What is happening to the world?" He had begun to resemble a maniac. "Is there going to be a war? Is there something I should know? Are we all gonna get fucked?!"

"No major war," I tried to sound reassuring. "Local conflicts, yes. A few thousand deaths, maybe ten thousand. *Their* deaths, not *ours*. Mainly in Africa, Asia and

Latin America. Nothing major. Maybe. We can hope."

"What about the Japanese?" hissed Green. "They think we are brain-dead. Today I read some statistics: over 60 percent of Japs don't think we are good friends and surely believe we are assholes. What if they talk to the Chinese? And how do we know they are not talking to the Chinese right now? And what if the Chinese confirm that we are assholes? Then what? They make better cars and CD players, their children have better scores, their buildings are already higher than ours. What will happen if they realize that they don't have to kiss our ass, anymore? What if they stop financing our debt?"

"They won't act on it too soon," I said. "They may act on it eventually but not so soon. And even so, they will need us to buy their goods."

"But what about Mahathir's trip to Osaka? Did you hear? He said to the Japanese: *Be our leaders! Be the leaders of Asia! Help us get rid of those fucks who are pushing their shitty Western culture down our refined Asian throats.*"

"He didn't say it that way," I smiled.

"He did. In his own words. Malaysian style. The Asian way."

I finished my whisky. The beer tasted awful.

"I think I know what you are all thinking. You think the allies will fail us."

"The allies?"

"Europe! The rich! You think people of the poor nations will take their knives, sticks, and hammers and come smash our heads. You are afraid of them."

"Not me, I'll move to the Yucatan," said Cathy who suddenly reminded me of the Countess. "Men in New York are sissies, anyhow. A beauty over forty can't find a husband. What husband? She can't even get laid."

"They will finally get us, won't they? They'll come here, they'll migrate, they'll infiltrate the entire country," insisted Green. "They might even bomb us one day in this very city!"

Bruce Springsteen howled something about an unidentified woman who had been shot point-blank, right between her eyes, while members of the proletariat attentively listened, sucking on their deadly poisons.

"I don't know," I said.

"It's all right with you, since you have friends among them. You have friends all over the world. But what will happen to people like me?"

"They won't get to the city for a while," commented Cathy. "They will first infiltrate the suburbs. In fact they may never get downtown. What would they do here? Hit Bloomingdales, go to the opera?"

"What are you talking about?" screamed Green in disbelief. "They are already here! Don't you see them every morning as they crawl from the subway?"

"Who are *they*?" I asked.

"The ones we screwed," explained Green, starting to bite the skin around his nails. "The ones they – the Europeans – screwed and we finished. Countries where we established dictatorships and trained death squads, from which we have stolen raw materials and destroyed labor unions, forced down labor costs, and ruined traditional agriculture. Countries where we helped to murder the secular and progressive leaders while supporting the religious fundamentalists, only so we could count on an obedient, brainwashed, and scared population willing to work for our companies for nothing. Not that I give a shit about all that crap, but I spoke to Moretti today..."

"That explains everything," I said.

"What?"

"Moretti is in *'zapoi,'*"

"Right," confirmed Green. "He is in *zapoi.* What is *zapoi*, anyway?"

I sighed.

"*Zapoi* is a Russian word," I said. "It is untranslatable."

"Try," demanded Green. "Everything can be translated."

"*Zapoi* is when somewhere in Russia one man buys a bottle of vodka and goes to visit his friend. In his friend's house, there is one more bottle, already in the freezer. Well chilled, preferably. Some bread and pickles are waiting neatly on the kitchen table. They drink both bottles and later finish all the wine and beer they can find in the apartment. When they finish later with all the perfumes of the host's wife, they bribe the pharmacist and get some pure alcohol that can be easily mixed with water or juice. Eventually they get to industrial alcohol or brake fluids that can be diluted..."

"Moretti just got out of *zapoi*," said Green.

"That's not surprising. Considering the circumstances and the excessive friendliness of the environment," I said.

"Right," confirmed Green. "And Kinsley wrote his report. Did you read it?"

"Which one?"

"The one about Saudi Arabia.... Kinsley managed to get drunk in some tea room in Riyadh. Later he took the taxi, demanding it take him to the whorehouse served exclusively by Saudi women," screamed Green.

"No," I said.

"Yes," said Green.

"Did they kick him out of the country?"

"Oh yes. After he got kicked out, he wrote a long article, condemning Saudi society, condemning its royal family, its government and above all the way Saudis treat their women. He also predicted that there will be a massive attack against the United States, led by Saudi citizens. And since Saudis are our allies, he foresees a massive government cover-up. It looks like a Pulitzer Prize piece."

"Well," I hesitated.

"Anyway, I talked to your friend Gino Moretti. He threatened me. He scared me. He told me that US involvement in Latin America will backfire. He gave me a lesson on greed and tequila. And PAN. He swore that the Argentinean economy will collapse and so will the Peruvian, Ecuadorian, Colombian, you name it. He threatened that the Bolivian poor will fight against the privatization of drinking water. He tried to prove to me that Chile – undeniably a superstar on the bleak sky of South America – is still run like a feudal hamlet, by a handful of fascist families. He predicted that we will sponsor a coup in Venezuela against Hugo Chavez and that we will fail. He believes that we will not be able to maintain control over Latin America for much longer."

"We always somehow managed," said Cathy. "Why not now? There is no reason why not now."

"There is," said Green gloomily. "Moretti says there is. The reason is that we are not thinking, anymore..."

"But we never were," Cathy smiled in amusement. "Nothing has changed."

"But they did. *They* definitely changed," whined Green. "They don't even like us, anymore."

"They *never* did. They never really liked us. Neither Latin Americans nor Asians."

"But now they read and write books about it!" concluded Green.

"Shit," said Cathy. "I didn't think about that."

Two more canisters of yellow foamless liquid landed on our table. Green seemed ever more delirious and apocalyptic.

"You are supporting them, aren't you? You and Moretti and Joanne and even Hide."

"Who do you mean by *them*?"

"Never mind," sighed Green. "Do you think Moretti is a Zapatista? Do you think he is paid by the Chinese government?"

“Green, are you losing your mind? You should switch to diet coke.”

“Yes, I think I am. So what? And what if the Zapatistas have a point? What if FARC and MRTA have a point as well? What if your buddy Sub-Sub Felipe has a point? You see, I’m not excluding that possibility. I’m trying to be open-minded. That’s impressive, isn’t it? Will it do me any good in the hour of final justice? Are they going to spare me when they arrive here to repay us all our pains? Tell me!”

I had to take a leak. I pissed facing a Solidarity poster and an old photo of the central square of Gdansk. When I came back, Cathy was caressing Green’s face. Green looked disturbed. He looked like an enormous, fat, ugly baby. Green was definitely the one who was rapidly falling apart.

“Don’t worry so much,” I said to him. “Things may look confusing but there is an order within every confusion. Everything may stabilize.”

“Nothing will get stabilized,” said Green in a defeated voice. “I don’t need novelists. I don’t need poets. I don’t even need scholars. I need dedicated reporters who can summarize, simplify, guide, explain, and above all reassure our confused, lost, lonely, screwed and basically unhappy readers.”

“Good speech,” said Cathy.

“Thank you,” he bowed.

We ordered more booze. Green accepted his drink like a marathoner accepting water mid-race. No, Green was not yet done.

"You did not read any poetry from me," I protested. "Not from any of the places where I've been working for *The Weekly Globe*."

"I am not talking about you," said Green. "All I am trying to say is that you nor any of you should try to explain to them, our readers, how things really work. They don't care. They don't want to know anything. Do not make their life too complicated. We are not a state college. They had a chance to learn things at school. Or on their own. They did not. Fuck them, now! Give them what they want and they'll give us what we need: $4.95 a copy. Every week. And the more they read us, the more advertisers will pay for our lunches."

"Makes sense." I tried not to be confrontational.

"Now back to the essence. I still think that you all know something that I do not. I feel panic when I read your pieces. I feel urgency. There is something there that I do not like at all. It's like you all see a giant enormous shit coming our way but you don't want to share the knowledge with me..."

"We don't see anything special."

"Did we fuck up?"

"Who?"

"We. The West. Europe. This country. The planet."

"Of course."

"Did we fuck up to no end?"

"Yes," I said. "But it's not news."

"Did we really entrust our fate to the lowest cast: to the merchants, to the sellers, to the elite market vendors? Did we really make heroes of peddlers? Did we trade our fate for their goddamn bank accounts? Did we send into internal exile people who may still possess a few leftovers of brains? Did we convince the whole planet that greed is good and that in fact nothing other than greed matters?"

"All right," I said. "Is this a question or a declaration?"

"Forget it," said Green. "Did we employ religions, propaganda, the mass media to spread the dogma?"

"Green..."

He wiped sweat from his forehead. Then he took a long and lonely swing from his canister.

"I am afraid of you," he admitted. "Of all of you. Of everything."

"You have no reason to be scared of us," I said, finishing my beer. "You can fire us. We can all be out of our jobs in no time."

"It would not solve anything. It would make things even worse. I can't tell you exactly why, but that's how I feel."

"Look, forget about it. I think there are more immediate problems that we have to face right now. I think the owner is pissing in our beer." I did not mean to change the subject but the stuff we were drinking was rapidly decreasing in quality. It had also changed color, becoming lighter.

"He probably is," admitted Green. Then he screamed at the barkeep. "One *Wyborowa* with cranberry juice on the rocks and two beers. And please don't piss in our canisters, asshole."

The barkeep was not thrown off balance.

"Whom do you call an asshole, you fucked up Commie?" he responded in a thundering voice. It was obvious that he had been listening to our conversation for quite a while.

"Whom do you call Commie, you suburban prick?" yelled Green, smashing onto the bar his Republican ID.

Suburban prick did not go down well with the right-wing proletariat. Until now, the rugged patrons had been sitting silently, minding their booze and heavy thoughts. Now they stood up. These were not small men. No sissies here. The barkeep slowly approached Green, a bottle of Wild Turkey in his hand.

"Out of my place, you little guinea cocksuckers," he whispered into total silence. "No fucking Castroites in this place!"

Cathy looked scared. She had never heard such language even during the colorful EBTs. She whispered into my ear: "They'll gang-rape me. They'll kill both of you and then they'll enjoy my soft perfumed yuppie flesh."

Then Green stood up. Despite the size of the working class crew, he still loomed enormous and imposing. "I said two beers and Wyborowa with cranberry juice on the rocks for the deputy DA person, whom you just called a little guinea cock sucker, dumb shit." He pointed his finger at Cathy. "I truly hope your immigration papers are in very good shape, assholes."

The effect of his short speech was great and immediate. Even the most militant workers sat down, not knowing what to do with their hands and eyes. Some slowly moved toward the door, accelerating as their foul breath met fresh air from the street.

"You bore," I said admiringly. "That was another typical filthy Republican trick."

"Give us a beer or we'll send you back to the Gulag," agreed Cathy, regaining her composure. "That's what you said indirectly. Clear blackmail. How politically incorrect you are, my love."

"Poland is not a gulag," protested Green. "Not anymore. It's our new ally, our great new friend, a member of NATO, an East European candidate for membership in the EU, a country that is attracting foreign investment at an accelerated rate. The centerpiece of New Europe."

"I'm not a deputy DA," said Cathy, softening. "I only said I work for the DA's office."

"I know," said Green, feeling proud and big again. "I needed to protect you from-"

"He needed to protect you from our readers," I explained.

Beer arrived and so did the vodka. The color of the liquid had substantially improved. There was even foam on top and no suspicious smell. It now even vaguely smelled like beer. The look the barkeep gave us was full of subdued hate and servility and fear.

Green kissed Cathy's hand. Touching. Very touching, indeed. I shut up, confronted with such great proof of gallantry.

Together, we finally adopted an optimistic approach to the world. Green grudgingly accepted that there would be no major conflict in the foreseeable future. Japan would stick to its cars and shrinking economy, its electronics and political scandals. China would continue with economic growth, cheap clothes and toys. The Prime Minister of Malaysia might even limit his anti-Western outbursts to private conversations over a nice cup of tea with the former Senior Minister Lee of Singapore. Poor people would wait too, choosing to die from starvation instead of destroying the tremendous accomplishment that was Western civilization, its dominant role in the world based on the wise and democratic principals of free trade, open markets, and globalization. Such a view of the future was mostly wrong or irrelevant but at least it had the advantage of being optimistic, for the sake of the rich world, especially the West.

We paid the bill, and then the Chief Editor of *The Weekly Globe* puked all over the sidewalk. Cathy was very nearly unconscious. I loaded them both into the back seat of Green's car and then drove them both to Green's condo, for offloading.

It was dark. A cold and light drizzle fell on the windshield. I drove slowly through the empty streets. I took the 59th Street Bridge and crossed back to Manhattan. As I cruised over the bridge, I was aware of the fact that this was still one of the greatest views in the world. I felt shivers down my back, and I had to swallow hard, because I still loved this city, enormous and proud and unplanned and fucked up but the greatest city on earth nevertheless. I did not wish to return to it to stay now, not yet, but the city would always stay with me, inside. I felt honored that I used to live here – no matter where I traveled, no matter where I lived, it was my city. It was indifferent, free of sentimentality and tenderness, with an enormous brain and an enormous engine, the product of millions of human efforts and of human daring and dreams, each dream different, so many efforts uncoordinated. It was the only truly cosmopolitan city on earth, embracing all cultures of the planet, not inviting much of anyone in these days and not trying to hold anyone in who did not want to stay, growing to the sky, leaving behind those who were weak, breaking them and crushing their bodies and their souls. It had never claimed to be a kind and gentle city. It was brutal and honest and it knew how to appreciate greatness and how to scorn mediocrity and how to ignore weakness. My brain revolted against its almost non-existent social concepts and its lack of compassion. But like the city, I also scorned the emptiness of commonly accepted truths. I admired those who refused not to dream, who still knew how to dream, how to be insane, how to create, and to dare, and to fly.

27

I woke up around noon surprisingly free of a major hangover.

All these years I had kept one room in a walk-up building on the Upper East Side. The flat belonged to another journalist who had been living in Paris. He came here no more than twice a year, as did I.

I looked outside – snowflakes covered almost the entire fire escape behind my window. I made a delicious espresso in an archaic machine bought in a second-hand store in Little Italy more than ten years ago.

There were two messages from Reiko. I read them carefully knowing there was no point in responding – she was already on her way to Bali.

I had waited for these words for almost a year, and now I was reading them and it was finally true. She had expressed her love for me. It felt as if everything had changed in the two minutes I spent reading her emails. But had it really? There was no joy in her confession. I guessed at her confusion between the lines. There was no determination in her notes – no willingness to act anytime soon, no concrete promise. She said, “I am afraid I am in love with you.” She was afraid. I felt empty.

Opening the window I was struck by the fresh cold winter air entering the room and I breathed it with pleasure, leaning on the frame, watching people walk on the wide sidewalks below. I tried to absorb the atmosphere of the city after five months away.

I left the apartment and ate breakfast in the Daisy Muse Diner, then walked west on 79th Street, all the way to Central Park. I entered the Metropolitan Museum of Arts. I used to go often when I was a student, learning about Chinese and Japanese painting and about the ancient civilizations of Central and South America. I had heard the Beaux Art Trio and Moscow Virtuosi for the first time here – in the discreet concert hall next to the Egyptian Section.

In the Museum Shop I bought a little blue replica of an Egyptian hippopotamus for Keiko. Then I walked without any plan for an entire hour inside the enormous museum, ending up in the section of ancient musical instruments.

I needed to meet with Moretti and Joanne and Hide in the early evening. Having plenty of time, I walked slowly down Columbus Avenue, all the way to the Lincoln Center. I stood for a long time in front of two of the largest paintings of Marc Chagall, hanging behind the front glass panels of the Metropolitan Opera. The paintings were clearly visible from outside. Many years ago, I used to buy standing tickets to the

Metropolitan Opera – for six dollars – hoping that the upper-tier seats would not be full and I would be able to move down once the lights were switched off. I would come here to dream, at least once a week, listening to the greatest singers on earth, using the opera as a background for my imagination. I had no idea whether a standing room gallery remained at the very top of the hall. Now, in order to get to the ticket office, one had to go through a security check. I decided to leave Lincoln Center after admiring the sad beauty of Chagall's canvases.

I caught sound and sight of a man standing on Broadway and 78th Street. He was in his fifties, wearing an old black coat, his beard long and untrimmed, his eyes looking straight ahead. He hollered out a monologue, while being passed by an indifferent stream of people. I came closer, curious.

"They will come unexpectedly, in the morning. They will use big jets full of people and fuel. They will fly them into the towers of our business center and into the Pentagon and White House. One target will be missed, and one target only. Relatives and friends will receive chilling final phone calls and electronic messages from the passengers on board those doomed jets. There will be death and destruction, fire and smoke. The towers will collapse and the horrifying images will be transmitted through satellites to every television screen on earth. People will jump from the windows of the burning towers, their bodies will smash against the concrete pavement far below. Thousands will die. America will be swallowed by fear, a fear that will be fed by rulers shameless enough to manipulate it to their own advantage. God's name will be used again and again, first by the attackers, later by those who will seek vengeance..."

I approached the man. I had never liked prophets, real or fake. I did not trust them. I did not believe in doomsday or conspiracy theories. Reality was bad enough – often much worse than any dark prophecy.

This prophet seemed different. He lacked fake conviction and he seemed free of arrogance. He spoke as if he were delivering a lecture on Dostoyevsky at a minor state college. The entire setup was thoroughly absurd. Yuppies in corporate uniforms spoiled the beauty of the Upper West Side architecture, Korean pop hits flew from the near-by deli, a lady in an expensive coat strolled her English bulldog. New York life flowed, uninterrupted. But here was this man predicting the disastrous end of two mighty towers – two great symbols of Manhattan corporate might, of US prestige and preeminence.

When he noticed my interest, the man stopped speaking, smiled, and looked straight into my eyes. He waited.

"How do you know?" I asked.

"I can't tell you," he said. "I wish I could answer your question."

"Who told you?"

"Nobody," he replied. "I know."

"But surely..."

"Nothing like that. No revelation, no dream."

"And when will it happen?"

"On September 11th, 2001."

"Do you know the hour?"

"No. I know it will be in the morning, in full daylight. Only that. I can see the planes and the people inside and what will follow."

"Why will they do it?"

"Because they think there is no God but their God. At least this is what they will say. And there will be other reasons. It's always about power, as you know. Not only on their part."

"I should get you some coffee," I said.

I went to the nearby deli and bought two cups of coffee with milk. I slipped a few packets of sugar into the paper bag. He might like his coffee sweet. The man took one cup and thanked me.

"Who are you?" I asked.

"A prophet," he said. "A new prophet. You know, I'm not alone, not the only one. There are several of us in different parts of the world. But I am the only one who lives in New York. I am the Manhattan prophet."

"A prophet?" I asked. "Of God?"

"Not at all," he replied. "Don't you know, it's not like that. It's not like people imagine. All these notions about God... The arrangement is very complicated. It's not as simple as people would prefer it to be. I can't tell you, I'm sorry, I'm not sure how to describe it all myself. I have an idea, but it's not easy to explain."

"Surely you heard it somewhere... from someone..."

"Nothing as simple as that, really. Nothing so simple at all. I just know. Things were revealed to me and to a few others. To be a prophet... It's almost a waste of time these days. Nobody wants to listen, as you can see. The TV preachers have spoiled people – they visit directly in their living rooms. And a great majority of them are fake, anyway. There is always someone predicting something. You don't get paid for prophecy. People are happy to ignore you. When what you describe actually happens, nobody ever remembers that you forecast it long before. But I have to speak. It's my mission. Although it won't have great results."

"His tone of voice," I thought. "He could have been complaining about educational reform, or the lack thereof."

"Drink your coffee," I said. "It's cold outside. You need something warm in your stomach."

"Very kind of you," he replied. "Very kind indeed."

The man's hands squeezed the thick paper cup. He took several sips, absentmindedly.

"So if nobody listens to you..." I began. He almost immediately interrupted, certain of what I would say.

"It's not that nobody listens. Those who matter do. You stopped, you approached me."

"I was curious, that's all."

"Sometimes it takes nothing more. Curiosity."

"Nothing more for what?"

He remained silent.

I observed him. He was not trying to convince me of anything. We were chatting in the middle of Broadway on a crisp winter day. Which was fine with me. I could be his singular audience for a few minutes.

"So what if it happens?" I asked. "What then?"

"You will have to decide."

"How so?"

"Decide what to do. First of all, don't get mad. Don't go mad. Too many people will be full of hate. Others will be crazy. You will need to think about what happened and why. Everything has a logic."

He pulled out a small piece of paper and pen and wrote the date: September 11th.

"The day of the Chilean coup," I recalled. "September 11th, 1973. One of the oldest democracies on earth was raped and ruined. In just one day. One of the greatest, one of the most beautiful countries on earth was fed to the dogs, because its people wanted to choose their own future."

"That's right," he nodded. "The very same day. Make sure you sit down and think things through after it happens. What you say now is a good beginning. Place this piece of paper in your wallet or somewhere that you will always be able to find it."

I did what he said. I put the small piece of paper between two credit cards.

"Do you need money?" I asked.

"Not really, no. I get by."

"How can I contact you, in case it happens?"

"Why would you want to contact me?" he wondered. "I'm a messenger, not a therapist, not a priest. When there is a need to pass another message, we should meet again, or you should meet others."

"But I would like to be able to..."

"Here," he handed me a simple business card with his name and telephone number. There was no profession noted under his name. "You can call me, of course. There is no harm in it. Try it. Call me."

"Do you have any religion?" I asked.

"Of course not. What do you think I am – a cultist? Even Jesus opposed organized religion. The Christian religion was created in his name but against his will. What people really need is to think, to not be gulled."

I shook his hand and wished him good luck. He smiled and waited a while and then again shouted his apocalyptic predictions to the crowd passing by.

I walked for a few meters, and then stopped. I observed him from the distance. It struck me that all he had said would actually occur.

I walked on.

On September 11, 2001, the blowback from imposing the US empire on the world would happen exactly as predicted. People would be surprised. They would wonder, "Why? How? Who?" Some might even begin looking for a prophet, a new prophet, and for new leaders.

I turned back to where the prophet had stood. I wanted to ask him another question. But he was gone.

28

I did not feel like going underground to the subway. I continued to walk down Broadway, from Columbus Circle all the way to the West Village. The city had changed. It had become much more segregated than before. No more of rich and poor folks walking side-by-side on the same street as before, ten years ago. The city looked cleaner and safer, but more bland and not so unique. Chinese restaurants had almost disappeared along with old-fashioned Greek diners and local pizza parlors. There were hundreds of overpriced Italian and French bistros and restaurants and increasing numbers of fast food joints. Now chains were appearing everywhere, like a plastic mold: fast food chains, bookstore chains, music store chains, clothing store chains. 42nd Street increasingly resembled corporate G-rated porn. New York was losing its uniqueness, slowly being converted into an "American" city, a corporate city.

I made it to the Olive Tree Café a little early. As always they were projecting silent Charlie Chaplin's films. I ordered *falafel, hummus*, and salad. Moretti and Joanne arrived on time.

Joanne wore a long Joan Baez style skirt and at fifty looked attractive and fresh. Moretti's hair was a mess, his black designer jacket wrinkled and stained. His Movado watch had cracked glass.

"Gino," I said. "You look like you were interrogated by the NVD for an entire week."

He winked and embraced me. He smelled like a strange combination of expensive aftershave and cheap potato moonshine. Joanne smelled as good as she looked.

I avoided alcohol and ordered iced tea to help recover from the previous night's libations with Green.

Hide arrived impeccably dressed and in good spirits.

"Everybody still single?"

"Yes," said Gino.

"Nobody fired?"

"Not yet," I said. "I spent last night drinking with Green. He is not going to fire us. He is scared of everything and everybody who is not corporate or the right wing proletariat. He is especially scared of world revolution and of Latin American peasants."

"Good," said Hide. "We will scare him even more."

"Karel is courting your countrywoman," blabbed Joanne.

"Do I know her?"

"Reiko," said Joanne. She pronounced her second name. "He is cheating on us by running travel stories for her magazine."

"I know her," said Hide. "I know her very well."

"Big mouth Joanne," I said. "How do you know all this?"

"I've heard the gossip," she laughed.

"I know her," repeated Hide. "Is it serious?"

"Hide, this is not very Japanese," I laughed.

"Is it serious?" he asked again.

"Yes," I said. "It is serious."

"All right..." said Hide.

Moretti flirted with a young Jewish waitress who blushed and giggled, embarrassed by his advances.

"What's missing in their lives is poetry," said Gino after she left. "They are all starved for poetry. This little waitress is dying for poetry. She doesn't even realize it. Nobody taught her how to read poems, nobody writes poems for her. Nobody brings her flowers. She gets banged during a one night stands and when she returns home, she feels like a sperm disposal rather than like a rose. I feel sorry for her. I am trying to give her a bit of my unselfish romantic love. That's all."

"You bastard," said Joanne. "I've heard all about your unselfish love."

"Gino has spent too much time in Russia," smiled Hide. "He is totally out of line."

"In the eyes of Byron and Shelly, Pushkin, Petrarca, Dante and Cervantes, there was nothing greater than being out of line. Honor and love were primary for both men and women, labor secondary. A feeling of security was scorned by many great men of old. Do you know why Russians are now in such deep shit?"

"Because they booze up and don't work," said Hide.

"Bullshit. Because they grew up on great poetry. Because they sucked it in with their mother's milk. There cannot be a country of great poets that is simultaneously a member of the G-7. Such things do not go together. Russians cannot change and conform. They are fucked. Discounted. Frowned upon. Kicked to the side."

"Good speech, Gino," I said, sipping my ice tea. "Except that Russians too are not reading much these days. So where do we go from here? Are we going to nationalize the television networks and order them to broadcast live concerts of Mahler?"

"Yes, what do we do? Hit the bottle, or join the winners?" laughed Joanne.

"I'm leaving," said Moretti suddenly serious. "I'm going. Soon."

"Where?"

"Back to Salvatore Quasimoto and Eugenio Montale. Back to Dante Alighieri, damn it! Back to the essence. Back to writing books and suffering every night from lack of inspiration."

"Do you need a roommate?" I asked, laughing.

"Let's all move to Gino's house of dreams and rediscover the essence," suggested Hide.

"Come," shouted Moretti, making one great operatic gesture with his hands. "You are all invited. Come and laugh with me at the pop-culture addicts, at women full of charm but lacking the ability to love, at human desires stripped of greatness, at mediocrity, at businessmen – banal shopkeepers elevated to aristocracy, yesterday's street vendors now franchising the world."

"It's not much laughable," said Hide. "Also there is a practical question: What are we going to eat?"

"As Garcia Marquez once said: we will eat shit," explained Moretti. "But we will eat it with style."

"I'm not sure that your path to greatness is very aromatic," said Hide.

"It's no path to greatness," protested Moretti. "It's a path to regaining basic human emotions and instincts."

"I will stick to good seafood," confessed Joanne. "Even so, it would be lovely to receive a poem or two once in a while."

"Somebody has to do business, Gino," said Hide.

"Yes, of course. A group of people that has no creativity and few moral scruples. I am saying that these boring and dubious people should never be glorified. All those stock brokers, financial advisers, managers – banksters –strip them of the titles they have given themselves, take away any linguistic niceties, and what is left? A stupendous banality, manifest in their simple and primitive desire to accumulate wealth, their autistic ability to sell more units and possess more power than others who are more human, and at the expense of everything else, at great cost to the people and the planet, to civilization itself. And what do we do? What do the educated idiots like us do?"

"We all wait for Gino to tell us," said Joanne.

"Ok, then. We are all forced to play their invidious game. We respect the phony prestige pinned to their glorified titles instead of laughing straight at their dumb faces. We even depend on them, and sometimes we are scared of them. We send them our resumes, our CVs, ask for their money to finance our projects because they are the only ones who have money to disperse. We even treat them as equals. Some of us eat dinner with them, these currency thieves, these cash hoarders. We invite them to our parties, something unthinkable in past centuries. Can you imagine one hundred years ago a university professor dining with a businessman? Or a fisherman dining with a shark. Now it's the norm, because culture and intellect have become nothing while bean counting has become everything. Do we not all know these strong-armed narcissistic crooks? How many times have we interviewed presidents and CEOs of transnational companies? Was there much inside their heads? Have they had anything coherent to say once we moved the conversation away from their limited field? Of course not. They are kings of a few fragments. They are lords of vast but simple and brutal swindles. They are the overseers of arcane kleptomaniacal transactions. They are the new conquistadors, lifting the gold wrought by workers, plundered evermore.

Let's face it, the titans of commerce and power are the same old slave wage drivers, the new plantation bosses. Some display artwork on their walls, as investment. Some go to opera once a month to be seen as something more than their narrow, thieving selves, and to try to shed their inferiority complexes."

"Are you really leaving *The Weekly Globe*?" asked Joanne.

"Probably. I don't want to end up like Keensley, and I don't want to end up like Green. What can we achieve by staying? Become the chief editor of the Globe at the age of sixty?"

"We can eat," said Hide.

"What about your stories?" asked Joanne.

"What about them?"

"Don't you like writing the stories of our times anymore?"

"I don't know," said Moretti, his face suddenly losing any trace of mockery or contempt. "Maybe. But there are fewer good stories around. And after all, I can write my own tales, in my own books."

Hide offered up a bit of old Japanese wisdom, he said, a wisecrack that nobody entirely understood but that made us all laugh.

Hours after sitting down, we ventured to *SOB's* on Varick Street, where an obese Brazilian starlet screamed out her soul to an upbeat samba. At two in the morning I danced with a tall girl from the Dominican Republic. At four we all went out and ate hot dogs on the street. We said good-bye and then it was only Hide and me looking for a cab to share. He was staying a few blocks from my apartment on the Upper East Side.

"Are you really serious about Reiko?" he asked.

"Hide, you keep asking me the same question," I laughed.

"There is one thing," he said. "There is something you should know."

"What is it?"

"I can't tell you, not now. Not like this."

"Hide, don't be a pain. Tell me. Are you in love with her, or what?" I kept laughing. "It would be a riot – out of all the women in Tokyo."

Hide was not laughing.

"Don't be silly. I'm not in love with her. And I can't tell you like this, out here on the street. When you get home, wait for my e-mail. Give me twenty minutes, then check."

"You're going to write me an e-mail?" I laughed, though I had to admit it was not natural but a nervous laughter.

"Yes, I will have to. I am sorry." Hide's face remained serious, almost stern. I felt my world beginning to break apart.

We flagged a cab. We rod in silence uptown. In front of my building, we said goodbye, nothing more than that. I reached my floor and went direct to the kitchen to make an espresso. I turned on the computer."

There was a message from Luz, one of the girlfriends of Carlos. I hardly knew her and I could not think why she would write me in New York from Lima. I clicked open the email and it hit me. I stopped reading and stared at the computer screen. Then I lit a cigarette.

Karel. I don't know what to say. I still can't believe it. Your friend and my boyfriend Carlos died last night. He drove to Barranco; he drove straight into the old wall not far from the bridge. On his table, he left a message for you. I quote: "There are substitutes for everything and everyone. But originals: both my land and Ana were all that mattered in my life. The land is dying and I can't bear it. My people are starving, living in humiliation. They are broken, unable to fight anymore. The revolution failed. Ana has been dead for many years now. I don't blame you for what happened because you didn't know and I didn't want you to know. Please leave Peru. For your own sake. And now please try to understand my decision. I'm not like you, Karel. I'm a cholo from those big mountains that you know so well. I may be a painter, but I am a simple man – there was always only one land for me, and only one woman. Your friend, Carlos." Call me, Karel. What happened? What is he talking about? Why did he do it? He was an incredible artist. And a man I loved. I don't understand. Call me any time, any hour. Luz

It wasn't true. I refused to accept it. I put my head on the table and stayed this way for ten minutes, half an hour, maybe longer.

When I lifted up, I noticed that a message from Hide had appeared on my screen. There were two attachments. I skipped the message and downloaded the first attachment. There was a big color photo of Reiko, when she was very young, sprawling on a white sheet. Naked, her legs slightly open, pubic hair clearly visible. On the second one she was touching her breast with one hand, while caressing her inner thigh.

I stared at the screen. I felt as if I were being hit in the stomach with a boxer's fist. I couldn't think straight for several minutes. The screen saver darkened the monitor. I hit a key and then another, and read the message from Hide.

Karel, I'm sorry. Forgive me for sending this to you. I don't know when these photographs were taken, but there is an entire set of them and every Tokyo journalist knows about their existence. It's an inside joke in Japan. Now that she is a very well known photographer everyone wants to see these images. Again, I don't know under what circumstances they were taken and why. All I know is that you would find out sooner or later. I thought it might be better if this came from me rather than from a stranger. Girls sometimes do silly things – for money or to be silly. She was hardly eighteen or nineteen when she let somebody take these photos. I have to warn you – these are the least explicit ones. You don't want to see the rest. Please, accept my apology. Hide.

"Thank you, Hide," I said loudly to the empty kitchen. "Fuck you Hide, and thank you!"

I dialed Lima.

"Yes?" she said.

"Luz," I said. "Damn. I don't know what to say. I'm so sorry. So terribly sorry."

"Thank you," she said. "Thank you for calling. It's almost four here."

"I know. Forgive me. I just got home."

"It's all right. I wasn't sleeping."

She wasn't crying. She was calm, maybe too calm. She was not the only girl Carlos had been seeing lately, but she had no way of knowing that.

"Did he die instantly?"

"Yes," she said. "He drove into the wall at high speed. That's what the police said. He died immediately."

"Shit," I said. "I just talked to him a few days ago."

"Karel," she said. "Who was that girl? Ana?"

"She lived with me," I said. "She was..."

"Was it because of her?"

"Luz," I said. "Look.... Really. No, let's not go there. Not now, anyway. Ana died some time ago...many years ago."

I was shaking. I did not know if it had something to do with nerves or with my body itself, but I could not stop shaking, so I hung up the phone and went to the bedroom and howled. There were no tears just strange sounds coming from my throat and I squeezed the pillow and hit the frame of the bed with my fist. The pain calmed me down, a little. Images of Reiko and Carlos appeared before me. I fell asleep at some point and woke up again then slept for a few more hours, afraid to wake up, afraid to face the world beyond the walls of the room.

29

Eventually I got up and wrote a short comment on Sharon and the death of the peace process in the Middle East.

I had to do it. I worked on autopilot.

I called Lima and talked to the family of Carlos. I talked to his mother. I offered my condolences. The connection was terrible and she could hardly understand what I was saying, which was good because I did not make any sense.

I called Sub-Sub Comandante Felipe to confirm the date of the interview in Todos los Santos. Then I informed Green that I would fly there in seven days. I wrote an e-mail to the countess telling her she could come along but at her own risk and cost. I wanted now to work, to move, to fill every second of my life so that I would not have to stop and think. I replied to every email that came my way, even the most insignificant and ridiculous ones. If possible, I probably would have replied to spam.

New violence had erupted in Ambon, and there was now regular fighting in Western Papua.

I filled a big cup with freshly brewed coffee and sat at my desk, trying to regain a sense of control over my life.

The woman I loved was married and had a child. Now I learned she had stripped, posing for a sex magazine, and maybe had done worse things. While this had been a mere moment in her life, apparently, today and from now on, thousands of men, all of her colleagues no doubt, would see her naked body on their computer screens. I felt my guts squeezed, as if by a heavy stone pressing my stomach and chest. I could not get the images of Reiko out of my mind. I felt both anger and concern.

I left the apartment and walked to East River Park, buying three coffees to go in a small deli on York Avenue. I found my favorite spot, sat down and lit a cigarette. From there I could see the Triborough Bridge and Roosevelt Island as well as 59th Street Bridge. The river changed direction twice a day depending on the tides of the Atlantic Ocean and Long Island Bay. I liked to sit here at times, listening to the cries of seagulls, watching old tugboats pulling enormous barges by rope.

One of my best friends had killed himself. I had not been able to see it coming. In San Bartolo I had felt something to be wrong but failed to meet him before leaving for New York. I felt responsible, guilty, endlessly angry at myself.

Here I was about to start spinning around the world again: Todos los Santos, the Middle East, Indonesia. Though I felt no real impulse for going to any of these places, I had no desire to stay in New York either.

I thought about Carlos and was sickened.

Then, images of Reiko floated before me. Not the images I had seen on computer, rather the memories of the weeks we had shared together.

The more I thought about it, the more I realized she had not invited me into her life. It was I who had stopped her in the middle of the National Museum in Lima. It was I who had impulsively asked her to be my wife without even knowing her name, without knowing anything about her past. I had said I wanted to spend the rest of my life with her after merely knowing the shape of her feet, the beauty of her face. She did not encourage me. She never asked for anything. She never promised anything concrete, and she never lied. She was somebody else's wife. She did not belong to me. She had not committed to me. It was that simple.

I thought about what Moretti said the other day: we only dreamed within the frames permitted by the society. We were hampered by the dubious moralities dictated by all the insane religions that had been screwing the world for millennia. We did not dare break free from what we were told we should feel. And now here I was applying that same bogus judgment.

Fine, I thought. If I really love Reiko, then none of this should matter. If there is baggage, then I'll have to carry it, no matter how heavy. Otherwise I'll end up like *them*, calculating, by way of programmed feelings, with a cheap and simplified concept of right and wrong. Otherwise I should simply run away, right now, outraged or humiliated, and forget about her.

Reiko was far more than a mess of old pictures on a computer screen. She had a complex past and present and future. She had her dreams and uncertainties, fears and desires. She was human. She held the key to my love.

Neither I nor anyone should fit and file her into prefab box, to be tagged and run along an assembly line to a predetermined fate. Doing so would be far more nauseating than viewing any skin shots.

They won't get me, I thought. I'm not going to dance to the tune of their corrupt chorus. I should not even be outraged. I should not be moralizing. I conjured Reiko's face and felt tenderness. I imagined living the days with her. If felt good. I thought again of the pictures and decided the pictures be damned, our lives lay ahead of us. No one had an entirely pure past. This was no century of saints and I myself was not remotely one.

It was getting late. I knew what I had to do. I went back to my apartment and called Singapore Airlines. They quoted me a monstrous amount of money for a last minute business class round-trip to Denpasar, Bali, but I booked it anyway and put some clothes in a small bag along with a camera. I was going to the other side of the world for a couple of days even though in less than a week I needed to be in Latin America – in Todos los Santos. The flight itself would take two days each way and there was no rationality in my action and this was exactly what I liked about it, to hell with rationality. If this is a final gesture, so be it. If this turns out to be the real beginning of my life with her, then the journey would be priceless. I flagged down a yellow cab and asked the driver to take me to Kennedy Airport. My head was clear. I felt totally free and in control of my life.

As I crossed the bridge, I looked back at the city. It had never seemed to hold me back, to stop me, to change my mind. It never seemed to judge me. It merely stood there, arrogant, proud, indifferent, cold, and yet full of promise, and beauty.

PART III

30

Fifty men entered a small village near Todos los Santos. They walked silently at two in the morning, covered by darkness. The entire village contained scarcely a hundred houses, inhabited by the indigenous. There was no vigilance and no police post. In the past, no protection had been needed.

For decades this place hardly appeared on government maps – too insignificant, too far away, squeezed between steep rocky hills on one side and a humid tropical forest on the other. The locals spoke their own language, barely understanding Spanish, mixing Catholicism with their own ancient beliefs. The village was miserably poor but nobody was starving. Families relied on their own traditional support system.

During the last decade, guerillas had periodically stopped in the village to rest and to buy food. ENLP men and women were provided a small barn and were served food and water. The rebels tried to explain their strategy and their goals, giving reasons why places like this had ended up in total misery. Despite that, only one local boy decided to join them, and even that had happened five years ago. This place never sided with the government or the revolutionary army. It had never managed to understand the terminology either side used. Its people knew how to fish in the streams and how to build humble huts, how to maintain fire and hunt for wild animals – they knew how to live or at least how to survive. They knew nothing about ideology and nothing about politics. When it came to religion, to them Jesus Christ was more of a friend, a bearded peasant like themselves who guarded them from the sky. They knew nothing about this God since their minds were not trained to think abstractly and they had a tendency to believe in what they were able to touch. They knew nothing about globalization and multinational companies, nothing about the revolution that was gaining strength a few miles from their backyard.

The fifty men who entered the village were all well armed and their bodies showed signs of long and rigorous military training. Their black leather boots were identical with those worn by the regular army, but these men were not soldiers. Some had tattoos engraved on their arms that moved each time their muscles flexed. They were from a paramilitary unit, a right wing private army, though some had just recently retired from the regular military force. Their main purpose was to defend the present state of the country, to protect the feudal and hierarchical structure of society. They were paid by the powerful landowners and businessmen in Todos los Santos and in the capital. They often killed and terrorized in ways that even the hardened and extremely brutal local armed forces might avoid.

They entered the village and spread out, moving silently despite their heavy boots and large bodies. Each of four paths that led to the jungle was secured by two men with machine guns so no one could escape.

The leader of the paramilitary group accompanied by five of his best men went straight to the house of the mayor. They kicked the door several times but there was no answer and they kicked it again and they leaned on it with all their force and it finally let go.

They found a middle aged indigenous man sitting at the dining table, his wife next to him. They kicked him in the stomach until he doubled and fell on the ground.

They dragged the mayor's daughter by her hair, a sixteen-year-old girl hiding in the small bedroom. As she stood in the middle of the hut, they began referring to every part of her body with the dirtiest words known to their language, touching her buttocks and breasts over her old fashioned traditional dress.

"Where are you hiding them? Where are the bastards from ENLP?" asked the leader of the paramilitary group, though he knew there were no guerrillas in any of the jungle villages, at least not in this area.

"They are not here," the Mayor answered calmly, trying to get to his feet. "They have not entered this town in the last two months."

They slapped his face. First lightly, then harder, then very hard. Blood ran from his mouth and he spat it out on the dirt floor.

"They have not come here for many weeks. You can ask anyone in the village," he repeated, and they hit him again and this time he fell on the floor and stayed there, motionless.

About this time, the local teacher dialed the number of the police station in Todos los Santos, using the only telephone in the entire village. He informed the men on the other end of the line that the place had been invaded by heavily armed intruders. The police officer scarcely asked any questions and after listening to the frightened whispers, reassured him that appropriate action would be taken in due course.

"If you don't come soon, they will kill us all," were the last words of the teacher. A few moments later, the police officer who received the call heard a banging across the line, then the loud desperate scream of a man, and then a long silence. The connection was cut off. The officer hung up, lit his cheap cigarette, and put his feet on the desk.

"It has started, coño," he informed his friend who browsed indifferently through an imported magazine full of exposed female genitals and advertisements for penis enlargement.

"When should we go there?" he asked.

"In ten hours, I suppose. We have to give them some time. They won't finish soon."

"Let's not hurry too much," he yawned. "We have to give them some time to enjoy themselves."

They tied the Mayor to the chair, sitting him by the table. They ripped open the girl's blouse and took off her bra, feeling her buttocks under the skirt. She was not screaming, her eyes intensively locked at some point on the dirty wall. She had no strength to scream and she knew what was coming. She had heard stories from people who lived in other towns in the area. They took all her clothes off and threw her on the table, her breasts a few inches from her father's face.

They hit the mayor again and again and his head fell on his daughter's chest and he felt the softness of her body under his burning cheek and as they held his head down, he could hear her heart running in fear and as the first man broke into her body, he heard her scream and he felt her pain and they made him stay like this, while more men came from outside and satisfied themselves between the legs of his only child. After a while the girl stopped screaming and her breathing became hardly audible, hardly detectable and he tried to breathe for her and this is how they stayed, father and daughter, for almost an hour, his face covered by the blood staining her chest, her stomach and legs covered by her own blood and by the sperm of dozens of men.

They undressed the old woman, and forced her to drink cheap alcohol that they found in the kitchen, kicking her buttocks, squeezing her sagging breasts, trying to force the bottle between her legs.

After an hour they grew bored and tired and they shot the mayor point blank in the temple, blowing off part of his skull. Then they carried the girl outside and hanged her, still naked and bleeding, from the wooden bar supporting the porch of the house. She did not die instantly, her body shaking in final agony, and they pulled her down by the legs, laughing and screaming final insults to her face full of pain and a look of embarking on a journey to nothingness.

Gunshots echoed from every corner of the village. Shots were sometimes accompanied by screams or simply by mortal silence. Those who survived said later that nobody in the village had expected to survive the night.

The paramilitaries drank all the alcohol they could find. They raped the women and children, urinated and defecated on food stored in the barns, used domestic animals as living targets. They took money and valuables, although in this village there was virtually nothing that could be sold for any amount. Finally they torched ten houses around the dusty square. Almost every man was executed. Eight children and fifteen women died, too. More died later in the hospital of Todos los Santos.

They painted "Death to the traitors of the fatherland!" on the walls of several intact houses, and next to it they improvised obscene graffiti.

The entire rampage took six hours. In the morning, exhausted and obviously satisfied, they left the village, singing old military songs, talking loudly to each other, recalling details of the night.

At ten o'clock, half an hour after the butchers had left, the state police reluctantly moved in.

That same night similar massacres were carried out in five other villages and towns in the jungle, across the bridge connecting indigenous land with Todos los Santos.

31

Word got out and soon all the major press agencies of the world carried preliminary reports of the massacre. In total, over 420 had people died in a single night and more were dying in an overcrowded local hospital and in primitive medical centers – understaffed and lacking drugs.

The President of the Republic cut short his visit to a neighboring country and flew back to the capital.

The Mexican government immediately sent two military transport planes with aid, a mobile clinic, and ten surgeons. The US State Department "condemned the violence in this historically peaceful country, our close ally, that lately has made remarkable progress toward democracy and a free market economy." The Americans immediately blamed guerillas for igniting violence in the region and for provoking an "undesirable and unfortunate reaction like the one that has recently occurred."

Some news reports explained that most of the paramilitary members had been trained in the United States during their years in the regular army: most of the money supporting these right wing death-squads also came from the north, and funds were channeled through the military and, some said, through the government. These reports were mainly printed in marginal publications – all the major newspapers in the United States refused to directly blame the paramilitary, army, or government.

At six in the evening, the leaders of two rival guerrilla groups met twenty miles from Todos los Santos and reached a groundbreaking agreement, creating "The United Front of National Resistance." Felipe was elected to lead the Front.

The government blocked the road between the capital and the province. It directed a heavy flow of soldiers and military equipment to Todos los Santos.

"We condemn the violence by an unknown group of thugs, but we will fight with all our military might any attempt by left-wing terrorists to destabilize our fatherland," read the official press release of the federal government.

Riots erupted in the capital city as university students clashed with police, burning cars and buses in the center.

Two key Ambassadors, one in Paris and the other in Tokyo, resigned from their posts, declaring that they would not serve the government which had sold out to foreign interests, and killed its own sons and daughters.

At ten that night, the country's most famous writer and the Nobel Prize laureate, was expected to deliver a speech supporting the government. After all, the acting President had been his close friend in childhood, and before tonight the writer was said to have never "meddled" in his country's politics. This evening, the sixty-five-year-old but still strong and impressive looking writer refused any make-up in the television studio and went live on the air wearing a stained white shirt. He stood in front of the cameras, the powerful lights bothering his eyes, no paper in his hands. His voice and image broadcast to almost every household in the country:

"Some of you have been reading my books for three decades. I'm grateful for your trust. As a writer I have always tried to concentrate on issues that are common to all humankind. A long time ago I made a choice not to interfere in the practical development of my country. I refused to comment on politics. I refused to take sides. Even when this country fought a bitter civil war, I remained silent. Even when progressive forces took power but were immediately destroyed by brutal intervention from the United States, I decided not to voice my outrage. I was wrong. I failed you all. I'm now standing here – my heart burdened by shame – asking you all for forgiveness. I was scared exactly like so many of you were scared, too. I was not brave enough to sacrifice my comfortable life and my privileges, my conferences abroad, my security as well as the security of my wife and my children. But now, let me finally speak, because to remain silent now would be worse than lying." He lit up a cigarette, ignoring the annoyed gestures of the producer. "The President used to be my friend, and this is the only reason they invited me to speak on national television. But we were friends when we were sixteen, when we were chasing girls and playing football on the same team. The world has changed. I don't recognize the world, anymore, and I don't recognize my former friends. I don't recognize the man who became the President of this nation. Those who invited me to speak thought that I would defend him, that I would try to calm this nation. I was told exactly what I was expected to declare. And as it is becoming so common in this country, I was offered money in exchange for my support of this government and this system. I refused money and I promised nothing. And this is what I have to say: What happened last night is the most despicable act of state terror in our recent history. And I am accusing this government of having arranged the massacre of almost five hundred innocent civilians. I accuse the army of treason – for serving the interests of foreign countries and foreign companies, instead of defending the lives of its own citizens. And to those who will soon decide to fight this terror, I say: To kill the murderer is not a sin. To fight, in order to protect the weak and the abused is not terrorism, it is a basic human obligation. And we had better remember that, because tomorrow, next week, thousands of our men and women will fight..."

At that moment the live broadcast was interrupted.

Late that night, Comandante Felipe sat by the fire in the middle of the jungle, surrounded by his men and women. For a very long time, nobody spoke. They watched the flames. New peasants were arriving at their camp from remote villages.

"All this did not come as a surprise," he said. "We were planning to take the bridge in order to prevent them from what they did this morning. We miscalculated. We were late. While yesterday we were willing to talk with the government, there is nothing we can talk about now."

In the heavy silence, no one uttered a word.

"This is the end of guerrilla warfare," he said. "We are going to open a front here. We are going to mobilize all men and women. We hope that new comrades will join us, and as we can see, they are joining us already. From now on we will fight them in the open. In five days we'll take the bridge and take control of the only navigable river of this motherfucking country. They have more men and they are much better armed. They have tanks, helicopters and jets. They have intelligence and logistical support from the United States. But they are rapists and murderers while we are defending our land. Our people have lost everything: first to the conquerors, later to the multinational companies and to the puppet governments that sold their souls to the foreigners. Some of us may die. Maybe most of us will, maybe all. We have no choice. It is better to die standing than to live on one's knees. And yet our real obligation is not to die but to win, for the sake of this motherfucking land which is so dear to us all."

It was a simple speech, he thought. Maybe not profound enough. No matter. His men and women were not going to a university exam. They were going to war.

32

The tremendous four engine power of a fully loaded 747 rolled the jet down the runway of Kennedy Airport. The jet lifted off all but imperceptibly from the runway, then made a slow turn to a northeast course toward the Atlantic Ocean. I sat in a comfortable chair watching a monitor showing the exact position of the aircraft, and myself, en route to the opposite side of the world.

If I were a simple person with an uncomplicated history, and if Reiko were simple too, things would be easy, now. Physical attraction and longing for companionship could be sufficient for growing closer and building a lasting relationship, I thought. As it was, neither of us had made things simple enough. We had both lived through serious complexity, to the point where we felt suffocated or torn by our pasts. Plus, our personal and social references were much different, in many ways. I wondered if my impulsive and passionate feelings for Reiko could be a real and final attempt at love, an effort to break from an unbearable kind of freedom within which I had foolishly ensnared myself these past fifteen years? Did I desire Reiko so very much? Or did I simply desire to belong to her, to belong to anyone I might find captivating, one way or another? Was I, deep inside, scared? Would I end up living my life at loose ends, forever? Living utterly free until I was finally utterly alone?

What did Reiko mean to me, what did I know about her? Could we really sleep together every night? And in the morning wake, to what?

The airplane made a stopover at London's Heathrow Airport where I went to the lounge and was stunned to see the BBC's live coverage of the massacre outside Todos los Santos – it seemed to be the only story.

I watched the images in disbelief, though my first impulse was to look at the departure monitor and find the first flight back to the American Continent, to get to Todos los Santos immediately, through the United States, through Mexico, however possible.

I called Felipe. To my surprise his mobile was on.

"*Sí?*" His familiar voice.

"I am sorry," I said. "I am just now seeing on the news what happened."

"Yes."

"Is the date still set?"

"Yes."

I could hear him breathing.

"The date is the same," said Felipe. "But this is a beginning of real war. As far as I am concerned, yesterday they declared the war on our people."

"Maybe we shouldn't talk..."

"Oh, don't worry. They know everything. They know all about us. Why do you think they have done this? They knew we would not be able to stand down, anymore. They decided to pull us into the open finally."

"You can't fight the entire army," I said. "And you can't fight the Yanks."

"I know all that," said Felipe. "But we will. Because we have no choice. They have left us with no choice. We may be hungry and we may stink, but we are humans while they are beasts. There have to be some human rules left on this earth. No brutality is great enough to make them reconsider their desire to control the world. But you should probably stay away. People will die. Many will. Maybe all of us."

"Do I still have exclusivity?"

"If you really care about it."

"I do. And I'll be there."

"Think it over."

"There is nothing to think over."

I had to get back to America as soon as possible. I had no more than twenty-four hours in Bali.

33

"No," she said. "It's not possible. You are insane. How could you...?"

She came closer and I took her in my arms, I pressed her body against mine. I felt calm, and I knew I was fine now and there was no reason to speak or to explain anything with words.

"It probably took you two days to get here."

"Almost two days," I said. "But does it matter?"

"How long will you stay?"

"One day. A few hours. I have to go back, to Todos los Santos..."

"Just one day," she said. "You came just to see me? For one day?"

"Yes," I said.

"Karel," she said. "Are you mad? Have you really come all the way to Indonesia solely to see me? You are mad."

We hired a car and drove to Ubud – to Cafe Wayan and we sat in the semi-darkness of the tropical evening on richly decorated pillows. Light *Legong* music filtered in, played not by an orchestra but by two musicians far away.

For years this village had been my second home. Now I had no time to explain it to Reiko. I could not take her through the back streets and alleys, show her secret unspoiled views of the river hidden in rich tropical lushness. There was no time for friends or art galleries, no time for anything.

I had written books in Ubud, working always at night, where the nights were long and dark and silent, marked only by the gentle sounds of wind pipes attached to roofs and by the endless songs of frogs and geckos.

Now we walked together, hand in hand. Reiko was enchanted with this place, and I was willing to share every corner, every small street with her, but the next day I had to go to the Americas, to Todos los Santos. I had to witness Sub-Sub Comandante's last attempt to reverse history. His men and women would be crushed by the regular army. Theirs was a clearly hopeless gesture but it would be done.

"Let's stay here," I said.

"You mean, forever? Can you really stay in one place?" she wondered.

"Yes. Maybe. It depends on the place. I could live here with you."

"Could you really?"

We drove back to her hotel in Sayan; to the *Four Seasons,* to her private luxury cottage overlooking the river valley, a place that I had told her about so many times before.

We made love, very slowly again, like the first night we had been together in Madrid, and I tried to pass something to her through the movement of our bodies and hands and lips, I tried to talk to her about long years of self-imposed loneliness and the unbearable burden of freedom, all that my life had consisted of before I encountered her, and about simple gratitude for simply having her now by my side.

I did not use words and I was not certain whether she understood. Maybe for her those moments consisted only of physical pleasure and I tried to give her plenty of it, but in return I needed more, I needed almost everything.

When it was over, we lay naked and tired on a white sheet surrounded by the tropical night and I pulled her closer to me and she put her head next to mine, on the same wide pillow.

"We could stay like this forever," I said.

"There is no forever," she whispered. "People age, they go away. In thirty years, in twenty five years I will be an old woman."

"It's not important."

"That's what a lover always says, isn't it?"

"I don't know. Have you had many lovers?"

"Not many. Some. Before I met my husband."

I thought about the photos, which hurt. I was not sure if it was right to mention them to her.

"Did they all say they wanted to stay with you forever?"

"Not all. Some did."

I lit a cigarette. I took her into my arms again, and it relieved the pain for a few moments, but not for long.

"You are the best lover I ever had," she said.

No, I thought. Not this rubbish. *I don't want to be your best lover. When you are with me I want you to forget everything: your past, my past, the entire universe. I want us to be more fully alive in the world.*

Instead of objecting, I smiled at her to avoid confrontation. Her presence here in Ubud was overwhelming to me. This abstract tropical village with little canyons and creeks, old Hindu temples and ancient legends often made me lose track of reality. I was exhausted now after the long flight. Absorbing the contours of her body made me wonder whether all this was still in the realm of reality or a crazy trick played by my imagination. The last day in New York had seemed unreal and so had my spontaneous decision to fly to Bali. Todos los Santos – the slaughter there more unreal, in its infinite brutality.

Ubud was hot and humid during the rainy season, and that was now. At night, dim lights of candles performed shadow play and the village did not seem to belong to living creatures but to spirits. Or maybe to both.

Ubud was changing, too, selling out to developers from Java, becoming polluted and chaotic, enduring its first traffic jams. New restaurants and shops were mushrooming everywhere, the dormant charm gradually disappearing. That was irrelevant now.

Although Reiko and I had not said anything offensive to each other, it felt as if something between us was about to break irreversibly.

"Are you angry?" she asked.

"Yes," I said.

"Is it because of something that I said?"

"I don't know. Probably not. But maybe. Maybe yes."

She moved closer to me, putting her head on my chest.

"Karel," she said.

I didn't move. Didn't say anything.

"Karel," she repeated with a certain urgency.

"Yes?"

"I wrote you a letter," she said. "An e-mail, right before I left Tokyo. I said I am in love with you."

"Yes."

"I'm Japanese. These words don't come easily to me. But it's true and so I wrote you a letter. Do you trust me?"

"Yes."

"Are you sure you trust me?"

"I don't think you ever lied to me about anything. There are certain things you never told me about. But I don't think you ever lied."

She slowly raised herself on her elbow, looking at me intensely.

"Which things?"

"Do we have to speak about it now?"

"Yes," she said. "Otherwise, why would you mention it?"

"Photographs." I said. "The photographs that were taken when you were about twenty. A photo series..."

She did not say anything for a long time. It was starting to rain outside, heavy drops drumming on the roof of the villa.

"So you know. And it's over now."

"No," I said.

"No?"

"It's not over."

"How can it be otherwise?"

"Does your husband know?"

She jumped from bed. "Karel, everybody knows, don't you understand? Everybody. Except my boss who doesn't know how to navigate on the internet. When he learns, I will be fired."

"Why did you do it?" I asked.

"I was nineteen," she said. "I wasn't thinking. They offered money and it was a very big sum and so I did it, thinking it would be printed in one issue of a small magazine. I was a good girl before, the one my parents were always proud of. I was sick of being a good girl. I wanted to live. Later, when I became a well-known photographer, somebody found this old magazine and scanned pictures and posted them on the web. Then it became the amusement of my co-workers. They sent the pictures to one another. They began to collect them. Don't you know that people like to humiliate other people?"

Her tone was bitter but to my surprise she was able to speak about it in detail. I moved to her and embraced her. She rested her forehead against my chest, squeezing my hands.

We walked to the terrace, felt the humidity, listened to a weakening rain and to the sounds coming from the tropical forest.

"Would you really want to marry a woman like me?"

"Definitely," I said. "I never thought I had met a saint. What matters is what is now and what will happen in the future. Nobody can undo the past."

"You will not be ashamed?"

"Never," I said.

Suddenly she squeezed my hand.

"I am scared. I feel something is going to happen," she said.

"What are you saying?"

"I have a strange intuition. Something will happen. It's us or me or you. Or somebody very close to us."

"You remember my friend Carlos," I said. "He died a few days ago in Lima. He committed suicide."

"Oh, that's so terrible!" she said, an expression of fear darkening her face. "So sorry, I remember him. Of course I remember him. He was so kind to me. But it's not him, Karel. No, it's definitely not him."

"Reiko," I shook her.

"I love you so much," she whispered. "So terribly much. I don't want anything to happen to you. To us."

"I love you too," I said. "And nothing terrible will happen."

Then she remembered.

"You are going away tomorrow."

"Yes, but..."

"You shouldn't go," she said and this time there was determination in her voice.

"I have to," I said. "Many innocent people were killed. My friend is planning to take over the city of Todos los Santos."

"Karel," she said. "This entire past year you were always talking about *us*. At first I did not listen, it was too abstract, too impossible. I was not in love with you, at first. Now I am in love and I am listening, but now it is you who are drifting away. When you say us, it means you and me. If no you, then no us. Then me alone. Do you understand?"

"Yes," I said.

"I have no right to stop you," she said.

"You do," I said suddenly. *Do it*, I thought.

"I don't think so. Just remember what I said."

"I will. I promise I will remember."

It was late but we could not sleep and somehow everything was fucked up again, fucked up to no end, and I was afraid of the unknown before us. There was an emptiness inside me. I could see the immediate future too clearly. I had to leave Reiko in a few hours, take several flights to the other side of the world, check into the hotel, interview several people, march into the jungle and be there when the ENLP launched its final attack using old rusty rifles and horses against tanks, combat aircraft, and helicopter gunships. It would be such a waste. Horrifying. I felt tired of everything: my work, traveling, my life, the world. I was tired of playing hero. Like everyone else I feared flying bullets, and I feared mortars and missiles attached to helicopters. I was afraid to die but even more I was afraid of being wounded, badly, severely. I could not say no, however, to Todos los Santos. Not at this time. I would have to go without exactly knowing why. I would have to go, unless Reiko ordered me to stay.

"Reiko," I said. "For almost seventeen years, since I was eighteen, I have lived alone. I can't bear it, anymore. Before you entered my life, nothing really mattered so much. It was my life and I cared only about living it, one hundred percent, fully. When I felt lonely, I wrote books or travelled to some far away, god-forsaken place. But now I know you and you are here and you are what matters and I don't want to go on like this, anymore. I know what you will say. I know your answers by heart. But isn't there something we can do? Soon. Now. Without waiting another year, two years, ten years! Before it's too late..."

"I don't know," she said.

"Please," I said.

"I asked you to be patient."

"Time," I said. "It's passing. Fast. I've learned its value. Every year, even every day and minute has its value."

"I know," she said. "I'm afraid that I will have to age. And die..."

"That's not what I meant," I said. "Damn it, that's not what I meant."

"I know. But it's what I feel."

"I don't want to waste our lives, not one moment. I'm insanely in love with life.

Desperately," I said. "I am obsessed with you and with *living*."

"Yes, yes, yes," she said. "Me too. And I love you and now I like to say it and I'm afraid of time and I don't know what to do and I don't want us to wait any longer but there is nothing I can do at this moment and I'm very scared and lonely and..."

I didn't see her face but I felt her shaking and her slender body naked, totally exposed. I felt tenderness and despair.

"Have you ever lived with another woman?"

"Yes," I said. "A long time ago."

"In Lima?"

"Reiko..."

"Tell me about her. I want to know about your life."

"She is dead."

"Oh," she said.

"It happened a long time ago."

"What was her name?"

"Ana," I said.

"How did she die?"

I didn't want to go there.

"Tell me how she died," she insisted.

"She brought a fuse to a bridge that was supposed to be blown up. Something went wrong. She probably didn't connect it right..."

"Sorry?"

"The bridge. It went sky high. With her."

"You must be joking." She looked at me in bewilderment.

It was certainly no modern day romantic Japanese fairy tale. This was probably not how a young Japanese woman in a love story would die.

"That's what happened," I said. "I had no idea what she was doing. Carlos and I drove her that night to the bridge."

"Carlos," she said. "Your friend Carlos. The one who killed himself three days ago?"

"Yes, look..."

She sat up in bed, searching for a cigarette.

"Karel," she said. "My love, do you realize that I am not alone? I have a daughter who is still a child. What are you involved in? How did he kill himself?"

"Does it matter?"

"Tell me."

"He drove his car into a wall. At night."

"He drove into a wall..." she repeated, inhaling smoke deep into her lungs, then exhaling it slowly toward the ceiling.

"That's all I know. He drove into a wall in Barranco. He died instantly."

"Karel, was your girlfriend a terrorist?"

"Terrorist..." I repeated the word. "Ana was a sweet girl.... A bit uncertain, very shy."

"Are you a terrorist, Karel?"

I stared at her in disbelief.

"I am a journalist, Reiko. And a writer."

"You said your friend was going to take the city of Todos los Santos. You said it just a few minutes ago."

"He's not a terrorist. He's a commander of a large guerrilla army."

Shit, I thought. This wasn't going the right way.

"Are you a Communist, Karel?"

I left my bed. I felt the cold marble floor biting my feet. I said suddenly in a very cold voice:

"Does it matter, Reiko?"

"I guess it does," she said.

I needed a drink. I opened the minibar and took a small bottle of liquor.

"You are married to a man who is co-responsible for the nightmare this world is experiencing right now. Did you ever ask him who he is before you married him? Does it bother you that because of people like him – distinguished businessmen – billions of people are living in a gutter? If not, then why are you asking me whether I am a Communist?"

"Karel," she whispered. "I don't think.... I'm afraid we are really not compatible."

"We are definitely not," I said. "And maybe that is why we love each other so much."

She did not answer.

"Reiko?"

"Yes."

"What's happening?"

"Karel, I have to raise a child."

"I know," I said.

"Karel, are they going to arrest you?"

"Arrest me? Why?"

"You are probably involved in something illegal," she said. "You are mixed up with terrorists."

"Sub-Sub Felipe is not a terrorist," I said. "The paramilitary is. And the government."

Then I realized what was going on. Since we had met, we had never discussed politics. I had no idea what her beliefs were or whether she had any. Obviously her husband had some.

"Reiko, what are you telling me? Do you expect me to join a golf club, vote Republican, and buy Burberrys suits?"

I noticed she wasn't listening.

"Did you know she would die?"

"Ana?"

"Yes."

"Of course not. Even she didn't know."

"Did you love her?"

"I don't know," I said. "I didn't think so when she was still alive."

"Oh. Did you ever love any other woman?"

"You."

"Any *other* woman."

"Not as much as I love you," I said.

"You had girlfriends?"

"Many."

"How many?"

"Many."

"Didn't you ever want to have a family?"

"Yes. With you."

"I mean before."

"Not, really. Abstractly, probably yes. But never with any particular woman I knew before you."

"Why me? Why do you want to have it with me?"

"I don't know," I answered honestly. "I just do."

"Karel, what did you do when she died?"

"I went to Cambodia. To the jungle. To interview the Khmer Rouge."

"No," she said, shaking her head. "I am giving up."

"Don't," I said.

She leaned on me.

"Was she beautiful?"

"Yes."

"More beautiful than I?"

"No," I said. "But she was beautiful and she had very sad eyes and I never gave her what she needed and I still feel devastated about what happened. Carlos was in love with her. Like I am in love with you. She was all that mattered to him. I never knew. He told me a few days before he died, before I left for New York."

"How awful," she said. "They both killed themselves."

"No," I said. "Ana died in action."

"I see," she sighed. "I guess I have to learn new terminology."

"Just bear with me."

"Is life going to be insane when we are together?" she asked.

"Most definitely," I said. "Never boring."

"You promise?"

"Promise."

"Will you teach me how to laugh?"

"I'll teach you now."

I tickled her underarms, and she jumped out of bed and ran to the terrace. The moon was high, the clouds were clearing, and we could see the river below. I hoped that from now on nothing would go wrong. I embraced Reiko again and spoke with some words that I had read in books but had never dared articulate before.

There was the reflection of the moon on the river and the night felt again like silk but it was heavy and more full of sounds than I could ever recall.

"I don't ever want to regret what I'm doing," she said. "Please let's not damage this. Please let's make an effort and not destroy it."

"We'll try," I said.

We fell asleep at four. At five thirty the bellboy delivered a fax.

"I'm sorry," he said. "But it seems urgent."

It was a fax from *The Weekly Globe*:

Karel,

Just in case you have forgotten that there is a whole wide world out there around you....

Demonstrators clashed with the regular army in Todos los Santos. 17 people are dead. Barricades are going up in the city and a crowd is burning tires and furniture. The United Front of National Resistance has not done anything so far. Why? It seems they are waiting for something. Peasants from surrounding villages are arriving on foot, by the thousands. The government has declared a state of siege. Street fights are ongoing in the capital. The land border crossings with neighboring countries have been closed. Only the international airport remains open.

Are you shitting me, Karel? Are you really in Bali? Now? Green.

34

Reiko changed her ticket, not wanting to stay in Bali alone. She had finished her work before I arrived and was hardly in the mood for sightseeing.

Her plane to Japan would leave in the evening, forty minutes before mine would take me to Singapore and then back to New York.

We woke up late. The entire previous night seemed unreal.

We were back at square one. I tried to tell her about my past and explain why I had chosen this kind of life. I tried to talk about how much I had underestimated the destructive forces of freedom, how absolute freedom in its extreme becomes absolute loneliness, I tried to explain that human beings were never meant to be free of all relations. I suppose I was mainly trying to explain it to myself.

And I tried to tell her that I did not see much sense in what I was doing, anymore. I felt I was standing on cliff and did not want to fall, but the ground was moving and I was not sure how long I would be able to maintain balance. Whatever I did, whatever I wrote seemed to make almost no difference. The rules were set as if by an invisible all-too-visible hand. Entire nations went bankrupt, were destroyed, passed beyond salvation. Huge debts were piled onto the poor, a form of fiscal slavery. There was no real democracy anywhere. Revolutions failed, one after the other. Nobody bothered with alternative systems – it was accepted that no alternative would be allowed to succeed.

I had chosen to stay outside the game, unwilling to become part of the system which I despised. With this decision came the voluntary lack of home and identity and country. Now, finally, I felt a need for a home or at least for an identity, even a need to have a country. Unfortunately all the choices seemed unacceptable. There was no place I could identify with myself. I had lost all my illusions after seeing the whole world.

Reiko took it all wrong. I realized that she was afraid of dealing in too many complex issues. She even felt threatened by the vocabulary I used and by the descriptions of the world and events I witnessed. Disturbing, threatening, the world I knew was too hopeless, too unsettling, too brutal.

I gave up after a while. I decided not to speak. My words were dividing us instead of drawing us closer together.

We drove to the beach, discussed Balinese culture, painting and music. While, I swam, Reiko strolled through the local market. Later, we had dinner and went to Ngurah Rai Airport.

I let it all go, hardly saying anything, drinking one cup of potent local coffee after another.

We passed through immigration together, bought a few CD's of *legong.*

I took her to the gate and kissed her and that was that. I wondered what had become of our past year together, if anything.

"I don't know what to say."

"Don't say anything, then."

She walked directly to the gate, passed the security check, and moved toward the airplane that would return her to Japan. She did not look back. She did not wave. She went straight in.

To her taste, between us there was too much passion, too much love, not enough harmony, too much turmoil. I offered her confusion and bizarre concepts about life. I brought her no security.

And yet, she had opened to me. And I was open to her.

I hardly understood anything. I stood there, thinking, fine, all right, damn.

35

"Ana, *querida*, have some more." I was cooking shrimp with white wine, gradually adding butter and garlic.

Carlos sat in the kitchen, stuffing himself with food, washing it down with a big bottle of *Cusqueña* beer.

Ana barely touched her plate.

She drank a glass of white wine.

She smiled at me.

"*Me amas*?"

"Of course."

"*Cuánto*?"

"A lot."

"*Díme cuánto*?"

I made an enormous circle with my hand.

"Karel?"

"Yes."

"I am scared."

"Why?" I stopped cooking and looked at her, surprised.

"I am so scared. So terribly, terribly scared."

I stopped cooking, took her in my arms, whispered some funny words in her ear, as if she were a child.

"Do you believe in God?"

"I don't know," I said. "You know I don't. Definitely not in the same God they talk about in church."

"I see. I know. Do you think He is good, the God? I mean, if there is a God?"

"Who knows. I suppose He feels like having a drink once in while, watching what's happening down below."

"Be serious. Do you think He can see us?"

"Maybe He chooses not to. I don't know. Maybe He is too far away."

We stood by the wall of the dining room. I held Ana while she asked me these strange questions. I did not worry because she often spoke like this.

"Would you pray for me?" she asked.

I laughed. "I wouldn't know how."

She wanted to say something but could not. Her blue blouse was freshly washed and ironed. Her clothes were old but always neat. She never accepted gifts from me. When I offered to buy her new clothes, she always refused.

"Hey you two," screamed Carlos from the kitchen. "Are we going? Are we driving to the bridge? To that mysterious appointment of Ana's?"

"You really love me, right?"

"But of course."

"And you would marry me?"

"Ana, we've talked about this..."

"I know. I want to know if you would marry me if you did not hate the idea of marriage."

"Most definitely," I said.

"And you would have a child with me?"

"Yes."

"Good," she said. "I wanted to know."

She took dishes and glasses to the kitchen, put them in the sink, and turned on the water.

"All right, let's go."

She brought along a strange attaché case. It sat on her lap the whole time I drove.

As we were about to reach *Chorillos*, Carlos exploded.

"Ana, this is nonsense. Tell us what it's all about!"

"Bug off, Carlito. Bug *off*."

"Ana," he said. "We are not leaving you there."

"Carlos," she said. "Grow up. I'm meeting a friend. I have to give him some papers. If he sees the two of you there, he will leave."

"What kind of papers?"

I did not like this Suddenly I did not like it at all. After all, this was Lima in the middle of the civil war. Anything was possible. Especially at night and in *Chorillos* which definitely was not one of the safest parts of this generally dangerous city.

"It's better if we stay with you," I said.

"No," she said. "You go home and I'll come back, soon. Please."

We left her by the bridge. She crossed it, reluctantly. When we looked through the rear window, she was already gone.

"Where is she?" asked Carlos.

"I don't know," I said. "It looks like she went under the bridge."

"I don't like it," said Carlos.

"Neither do I."

We parked the car a few hundred meters from the bridge.

"Now what?"

"We'll go out there," said Carlos. "We'll wait for five minutes and if she doesn't come back, we'll search for her."

We waited in the car, smoking. We waited for two minutes and then all hell broke loose. The explosion was so powerful that it pushed our car forward. For several seconds we couldn't see anything, debris and dust flying. Dark and gray. The sound was deafening.

Then slowly everything quieted. There was no bridge, anymore. Nothing but an approach road and pieces of metal and concrete oddly sticking out from it.

At first we did not connect the explosion to Ana. We abandoned the car, running toward what was left of the bridge. We looked down, but nothing seemed alive. Nothing human, nothing that might resemble her, or anyone.

Carlos pointed into the semi-darkness below. I saw a rug, something that could have been blue but now was dark, soaked with liquid.

"Let's go!" screamed Carlos.

We heard sirens approaching.

I couldn't move.

"Let's go," repeated Carlos with great urgency. "Go, damn it!"

I moved slowly, automatically.

We got into the car. We flew through the dark streets of Lima, toward Miraflores.

"It was a fuse," said Carlos, all fucked up, his voice shaking. "She carried the fuse in her case. She connected it down there. Something went wrong."

"Shut up!" I screamed at him.

We came back home. We drank all the beer there was, we drank everything in the house. We did not speak because there was nothing to speak of. We fell asleep at five in the morning sitting in place, our heads on the table.

In the morning it took me a few minutes to remember all that had occurred the previous night. I had a terrible headache. Carlos was gone, and there was no message from him on the table. The clock on the kitchen wall showed two in the afternoon.

In the bathroom, I undressed methodically, entered the shower, and stood under the stream of hot water for what seemed like an hour.

Late in the afternoon I dressed and drove to police headquarters. I asked to see the colonel of the anti-terrorist investigation unit whom I knew and had interviewed several times in the past.

"You look like shit," said the colonel instead of greeting me.

"How do you expect me to look," I said. "You know what happened last night, don't you."

"I do," said the colonel. "I really did not expect to see you here."

I sat at the table. We both lit cigarettes.

"We identified her body. Or what was left of her body."

We watched each other, waiting.

"Now listen to me, pal," I said to the colonel. "Listen very carefully. Nothing, and I mean absolutely nothing, will happen to her family."

When you cover a war, it is always wise to have a few "bargaining chips" – in case you need to get yourself out of terrible trouble. You have to be able to defend yourself. I had lived in Peru for nine years. I had taken care to look after myself.

The colonel was waiting.

"You know me," I said.

"I do," said the colonel.

"You know me very well, don't you?"

"I do," said the colonel.

"You know how I can fuck you. How terribly I can fuck you if anything happens to them. You know I can fuck you so terribly that you will be shitting blood for the rest of your life, shitting it for so long that you forget all about your sisters and mother and all the rest of your family. You know that if I have to, I will fuck you so bad that you will wish that you were never born."

The colonel made a weak attempt to speak.

"No," I interrupted him. "Wait. And you of course know how I will do it if I have to. I will denounce you. I will denounce you for Abancay and for Alta Huayaga, for all these things you know that I know. And there is a file right now in Reuters and they will open the file if you blow out my brains right now, right here. There are tapes and negatives and some eighty pages of investigative journalism."

"All right," said the colonel. "What do you expect me to do?"

"Nothing," I said. "Absolutely nothing, pal."

"You know she had two brothers and four sisters. What am I supposed to do? Let them go? There is a great probability that they are part of the movement."

"You leave them alone," I said. "Especially the women because both of us know what you do here with the women. But you will also leave the men alone."

"All right," said the colonel. "What about you? Did you know?"

"Of course I didn't know, *coño*. If I had, we wouldn't be sitting here right now. I wouldn't have driven her to the bridge. And she would be alive and that fucking bridge would be standing in that motherfucking *Chorillos*."

"Let's suppose it's true..."

"You know it's true."

"Karel," said the colonel. "Your fiancée, your girlfriend blasted the bridge. Big bridge. Sky high. She was a Shining Path member. Her family is probably involved big time. You drove her to the bridge, and, then, right after that, it went sky high. Are you insane? What am I supposed to do? We are fighting a war."

"You are fighting a dirty war," I said.

"Can you stop fucking up, Karel? Have you come to deliver a speech in defense of the Shining Path here in this anti-terrorist headquarter?"

"I am not defending them. They are the same motherfuckers that your men are. All I am telling you is that you will not touch her family."

"Karel," said the colonel, "I have to arrest you."

"Very well," I said.

"All right. You are officially under arrest. I will interrogate you now. Well, it's what I am doing at this moment, anyway. You will have to sign some papers. We'll write a protocol. After one hour I will release you because of lack of evidence."

"Her family," I said.

"What do you have on Alta Huayaga?"

"Two villages your men rampaged. Random executions, two hundred-fifty rapes, one of them of a seven-year-old girl. Of course drugs. Your men are trafficking..."

"All right," said the colonel. "Do you have tapes, negatives, everything?"

"Yes."

"I want them all."

"What will I have left?"

"Evidence on Abancay. And my word."

"I trust you."

"And you will never publish one word about that incident as long as I live."

"Fine," I said.

"Do you really think I'm a monster?"

"No," I said. "I know you. You are a mere opportunist, not a monster."

"Karel," he said. "I studied five years in London. I wanted to be a good cop. I tried to outwit my adversaries, I really tried. I hate violence. I never touched one prisoner, I never tortured anybody, damn it."

"I know," I said. "But you are still here. And your men are murdering and raping."

"I have hardly any control over them. This is a wild country, Karel."

"Colonel," I said. "Let's not get into this. The main thing is that we agree..."

"We agreed," said the colonel. His impressive, robust figure rose from the chair. He stood behind the table, staring straight into my face. His eyes were cold, piercing and unpredictable. If he would point the gun at me, if he would shoot me point blank, I would not be surprised...nor if he tried to embrace me. Instead he smiled, suddenly. "Now, in order to seal it, we'll go and get some whores."

"Right," I said. "We'll seal it."

"You are paying. I want blondes, first class, from San Isidro. I choose."

At eight we left Headquarters and drove to a San Isidro strip joint where the colonel selected two women.

"You'll need one, too," he said.

We rented two rooms. I went upstairs with one of the girls whose name I could not remember. She undressed in the darkness and I lay down next to her, still fully dressed, and she kissed me on the lips and called my name and I felt her hand on my hair and she said things she was supposed to say but I was only lying on my back, everything empty and broken inside and I turned toward her and saw her large breasts in the semi-darkness which my eyes were adjusting to, and then I recalled that I had not cried in a long time, since I was a child, but now I was crying. She raised herself on her elbow:

"*Qué te pasa, chico*?"

She touched my face.

"Tell me."

And I told her all there was to tell. And my words poured out like blood, like vomit, like tears. I told her everything and she pulled my head on her breasts and I felt her softness and as I spoke she caressed my hair and I spoke about Ana and so many other things I had never dared to speak about to anyone else before and she kept caressing my hair, repeating kind words pronounced in a soft, healing voice, and I couldn't stop, I felt my own tears, a long forgotten sensation. I was crying for Ana, for myself, for Lima, for Peru, and for this young woman as well.

"It's all fucked up," I said wiping off tears from my face. "All fucked up."

"Yes," she said. "All fucked up. But you will leave now and in one month, one year everything will be all right again for you. You will forget. Wounds will heal. There will be another girl, another woman. Another love. As for me, I will stay."

"Forgive me," I said, because I knew she was right.

"Don't cry," she whispered. "Boys don't cry."

"I know," I said. "I never do."

We embraced. We sat on the old bed of the cheap one-hour hotel in San Isidro brought together briefly by chance, by war. Empty from pain and fear, wishing now to gain strength from each other, scared of the night, scared of the future and a terrible emptiness brought on by nothingness and despair, we sat together without moving for a long time.

"*Soy Monica,*" she said, and her voice was as sad as a bass sax. It was the blues.

I would convert her voice to music and climb to the top floor and blow it out over the roof to cry as only blues can cry, and make it fly over this tremendous city of insanity, pain, war, solitude – if only I could have.

And I wanted to pay a tribute to the girl I had really never loved but whose presence I missed now incredibly, the girl who slept in my arms for a year, ultimately wanting to be my wife, a woman who was scared to die and then perished with dignity and with honor, if for confused or unreachable dreams.

"Do you hear me, Ana?"

I stared into the dark sky of Bali through the windows of Ngurah Rai Airport.

"Ana..."

But there was silence.

And then a roar of engines. The DC-10 of Japan Airlines, rolling on, toward its own point of no return on the runway, taking off, turning toward Tokyo, Japan. I watched its green and red strobe lights disappear into the clouds.

"Fucked up," I whispered. "All fucked up."

PART IV

36

Gino joined my flight in London. I had refused to go to Todos los Santos alone and I had refused *The Weekly Globe*'s offer to send a photographer. I called Green from Denpasar and asked him to get Moretti from Moscow to London on the first available flight. At this point I had the upper hand – an exclusive for the biggest international story now playing across all the major media in the world.

Green reacted immediately, paging Moretti, sending him straight to the airport with only an hour's notice.

The Weekly Globe tripled our life insurance, but we couldn't think who to designate as beneficiary.

"I can't give two million dollars to some Russian whore," said Moretti. "Do you know somebody who needs money?"

"No," I said. "Not really. Those who need money badly don't have a mailing address."

"How is Reiko?"

"Fine," I said.

"Did you break up?"

"I don't know," I said. "It doesn't look good."

Moretti took a sip of cognac.

"Let me guess. She went home to Japan and you are going to Todos los Santos," he laughed.

"I suppose so."

"I see," Moretti finished his glass. "You know what? I think I need a woman who will tell me: Gino, you asshole, don't go to these places anymore. Stay home with me – to hell with the money. To hell with the glory, too. When I meet such a woman I'll probably settle down for good."

"If she looks like a model," I added.

"You know what?" Moretti smiled. "Not really. It's not a condition. Nice, yes. Nice body, nice face. Latin, Asian perhaps. But she has to say these magic words: Gino, asshole, don't go anywhere."

"And would you stay?"

"Oh, yes. Of course I would. But at this point it doesn't matter, anymore."

"Why doesn't it matter?" I wondered.

"Because we're going to Todos los Santos," he said.

We fell silent, buried in the comfortable seats of Singapore Airlines business class.

I finished *The Economist* and the *London Review of Books*, *The Guardian* and the *Herald Tribune*, and I read the *New Left Review* from cover to cover.

I also finished Hanif Kureishi's *Sleep With Me*, which was pleasantly depressing. I often felt that Kureishi was past his prime but he remained pleasant reading him on planes.

I started long journeys loaded with new books that I would buy in Santiago and New

York, Singapore, Hong Kong, or London. I shed books as I went, leaving finished ones in airplanes, hotels, anywhere, bringing only the best in my suitcase back to my library in Lima.

Books were becoming meaningless, too, as bookstores were swallowed by chains. Publishing houses increasingly resembled any other large corporation. As in Hollywood films, the plots of popular novels had become elaborate and forced, remote from reality. Writers had become pricey entertainers and buffoons.

It seemed that all that was left were the wrinkles on the faces of *literati* baby boomers. Once they hit fifty they got very scared, writing intensely about aging, erections, and bittersweet affairs.

Writers and their books used to present real opposition and expression against brutal oppression, injustice, and fanaticism. Great writers and their books could bring down kingdoms, religions, states. Writers and poets were as much respected as they were feared, their stories and verses sent entire nations to the barricades. In the darkest days of human history, certain books were among the only islands of sanity, nearly the only hope, the only place where one could search and encounter truth.

The new rulers had conquered storytellers and their books, bribed and bought them as if purchasing any other merchandise. Using writers, the owners of the world bought and sold the truth, wrapped it in a shiny package, and put colorful ribbons on top. Processed, reshaped, modified, smoothed, and beautified, the truth, in its new form, was marketed and sold, passed off as culture or pleasure, or sheer exploitation.

In these stories of the corporate age, deep into the era of mass public relations, war was called peace, aggression was often labeled as defense. Brutal military regimes were described as emerging democracies, the starvation of millions of people was passed off as necessary austerity measures and wise economic policies.

Thinkers were locked up in universities – institutions reshaped to increasingly resemble huge companies and investment houses that happened to sell, among other things, education – their voices hardly audible, with hardly any influence on the daily life of the world.

Rebels were transformed into hollow stars, eccentric beings who would once in a while organize rock concerts and elaborate dinner parties to aid the impoverished parts of the world, while ignoring the owners of the world much closer to home who were energetically ensuring that the impoverished would always be there for the wealthy of the world, those who had helped to create much of that poverty in the first place.

Market fundamentalism – its dogma and practical applications – was defended like a medieval castle. The crushing centers of power were hated by the silenced majority of the world and could almost never be directly challenged. Many people had slowly accepted what would have been unthinkable forty years ago – that there were no real alternatives to the present system. Hundreds of attempts to challenge the direct control of this order had failed, were crushed, from Latin America to Egypt, from Indonesia to Western Europe.

For the first time in modern history, accomplished novels and poems were silenced on these crucial matters. There were no opposition writers in literature with much of any prominence. A dictatorship of corporate priorities had put them down, pushed them out, and helped others more amenable to the new narrow rules and roles of authors. First, one must stop dreaming about a better world. Some of those who accepted became rich. Others who refused, lived in internal exile.

Two years ago I met the famous novelist Arundhati Roy in the coffee shop of Park Hotel in Delhi. What was supposed to be a short encounter became a few hours long heated discussion. We discussed politics and we discussed the mounting problems in India, but we also talked of the state of literature, a topic about which we both felt passionate. We agreed that almost all great contemporary writers seemed to be lethargic or asleep or were too frightened to address important global issues. Or maybe there were almost no great writers left.

Philosophy, politics, social criticism, and vision were replaced by frivolous, entertaining plots. The pitiful state of today's world, its disparities and scandalous post-colonial, corporate-dominated arrangement topped the list of some of the issues hardly discussed on the pages of contemporary novels. Fiction had become politically and socially detached and therefore historically and morally irrelevant. Instead of aiming at retaining their status as "the conscience of society," most writers opted for much more modest goals, turning themselves into entertainers and showbiz figures.

Great nonfiction writers were still around, writing brilliant books in the West, in India, in Latin America, but the novel, a literary form so dear to both of us, seemed to be finished, sold out and stained by an apparent – although somehow hesitant – collaboration with the financial and commercial interests of those who ruled our societies.

We parted in front of my hotel. I gave her a gift – a silk scarf from Vietnam – she gave me a hug, then entered her little beat-up car and drove away. I waved for a while, standing on the pavement, overwhelmed with absolute certainty that she was one of the bravest writers of our time.

Since then I have not had a chance to meet her again, but while working in the South Pacific I came across an issue of the Australian magazine *The Bulletin* that carried a long article on Arundhati Roy by Jennifer Byrne: "...I'm actually a writer, and this is what writers do and have done through centuries – commenting on the societies in which they live. But now because writing and literature has become a kind of quote unquote commercial activity, it's dumbed them down like nothing ever has before, so we are supposed to be some kind of court entertainers."

Ms. Byrne asked whether there was really such a tradition, or was she just being wishful? "Yeah, there was," answered Arundhati Roy. "Who were Sartre and George Orwell? And today it's reduced to something almost like toys, not even rigorous in your analysis. I mean who are the big writers today who have taken on what is huge in the world? Very few – unless they are on the other side. Like V.S. Naipaul commenting the other day that Saudi Arabia and Iran should be destroyed."

How could one disagree with Arundhati Roy? Of course such a tradition had run for centuries, helping humanity move forward. The greatest writers stood at the vanguard of the struggle against racism, colonialism, and imperialism. They promoted social justice, fought for changes. Romain Rolland, Anatole France, Emile Zola, and Maxim Gorky had placed themselves on the side of exploited, enslaved human beings, demanding immediate change, even revolution.

George Bernard Shaw – probably the greatest modern British playwright – had consistently ridiculed capitalist dogma, and his German counterpart – Bertolt Brecht – had openly called to arms against it.

An entire generation of outstanding novelists and thinkers wrote in postwar France: Jean-Paul Sartre, Albert Camus, and Simone de Beauvoir to name a few. All three had been active members of the anti-fascist resistance. All three had condemned the postwar arrangement of the world. In those days, philosophers and writers were not confined to university campuses: when Sartre addressed workers at a Renault factory, his speeches drew to the premises hundreds of thousands of men and women who had no problem understanding what he was talking about.

There were great novelists like Andre Malraux, Ernest Hemingway, and Saint-Exupery (author of a famous philosophical book for children and adults – *The Little Prince*), writers who fought in wars, engaging themselves not only by words but also by deeds. And their books sold millions of copies, despite the complex and often controversial topics they addressed.

In the United States, Richard Wright shocked readers all over the world with his novel *Native Son*, a damning, powerful and honest account of racism and discrimination against African Americans. A few decades later, Joseph Heller described the insanity of World War II in *Catch-22* and later the hypocrisy of corporate America in *Good as Gold*.

Latin America offered some of the greatest novelists of the 20th century: Carlos Fuentes, Alejo Carpentier, Gabriel Garcia Marquez, and Manuel Puig from the left, as well as Jorge Borges and Maria Vargas Llosa from the other side of the political spectrum. In Africa, Acebe described the destruction of local cultures by colonialism in his novel *Things Fall Apart*, while the Indonesian

Pramoedya Ananta Toer defined brilliantly the painful process of the birth of the young nation and its horrific downfall after the fascist coup in 1965.

These were just a few examples from the past, and the list was endless. The fact is that almost all great literature since ancient Greece has dealt with the most important issues facing humanity: from Homer to Victor Hugo to Franz Kafka to Albert Camus. That the most accomplished contemporary writers stubbornly refused to address the serious problems of the world was a disturbing anomaly, an exception from the historic rule, proof that something had gone terribly wrong, not least in the societies that proudly claimed their intellectual brilliance.

I felt like summarizing. I asked for cognac and a coffee. I found a pen and grabbed a vomit sac, and began scribbling. The airplane's puke bag as notebook – it seemed more than appropriate for the topic at hand.

The world is full of tremendous stories. Global market fundamentalism and neoconservative culture are overthrowing the democratic principles for which humanity has fought for centuries. Millions of people are dying having no access to medicine, while pharmaceutical conglomerates (backed by the governments of rich countries) are blocking developing nations from producing cheap drugs that would save their men, women, and children.

Humanity is suffering new colonial wars as well as religious and business extremism.

Congo has lost more people than any other nation in the world since WWII and the West fuels its civil war with absolute impunity. While our retirees get fatter and fatter gobbling snacks and beer in front of their TV sets, skeletal children and raped women with swollen wombs fill the already overcrowded camps around Goma. How many people from the 'educated' western nations have ever heard of Goma? Do they know the capital of Congo? What the hell do they know about Congo, about the Democratic RC? They should know, because Congo and other places like it feed them, pay for their early retirement, their unemployment benefits and medical care. 7 million people gone in Congo, to satisfy our hunger for their natural resources. All of West Africa in flames, people starving, dying in agony, so we can live luxurious elegant lives. Small island nations may soon disappear due to global warming – due to the unbridled consumption of nations thousands of miles away. Entire nations with their beautiful atolls, languages, music, stories. Gone.

I left my seat and went to bathroom is search of more vomit sacs for my outburst 34,000 feet above ground. Once resupplied, I ordered more coffee and continued.

There are great stories all around, across the globe. There is confusion and dissatisfaction in many developed countries, and there is anger and growing resentment toward the rich world in most of the desperate nations. There is the impotence of the poor and the spite of the rich that would make for great classic dramas or novels. In many poor places, medieval forms of religions shamelessly fill the void created by the systematic destruction of social movements and progressive governments. These countries are worse than poor, they are impoverished, having been made poor or kept poor by the wealth of the world, often by the wealth of the West. The West of course typically supports religious buffoons – for fun? no – for their oppressive utility. Our neo-colonialism, our mighty corporatism, our financial hegemony, needs obedient populations, slaves ideally. If the masses do not rise against the fascist preachers, how likely are they to fight against the grotesque and lethal, that is, unequal, distribution of wealth? What a story: what a powerful drama to write!

Great stories are plentiful: they offer themselves in the desperate shantytowns of Lima and Jakarta, in the fast-food restaurants and sweatshops in the US where broken men, women, and children labor at minimum wage, in the battlefields of the Middle East, Southeast Asia, and Africa, in the indigenous huts of Mexico, Bolivia, and Guatemala as well as in the small island nations of the South Pacific that are slowly but irreversibly disappearing from the face of the earth.

These are stories of monumental proportions, honest and good stories, stories that terrify while evoking compassion, stories that call for action – stories that the novel as a form is capable of telling.

If there is no lack of great stories, then is there a lack of great writers? Or have they been silenced, sidelined, marginalized? Have they been broken and starved, or forced to accept a regular job that allows them to survive but prevents them from writing? Have they sold out, writing romance novels and self-improvement books, producing hundreds of pages describing getting old or trying to solve a spectacular but irrelevant criminal plot?

I stretched. I was fed up. My scribbling covered several vomit-sacs. I placed them between the inflight magazine and the duty free catalogue of Singapore Airlines. Not in the best company but so what.

There are still great novelists left, I thought. Not many, but a few. Jose Saramago, Arundhati Roy, Tariq Ali, even Salman Rushdie who is currently levitating in a spacey, outlandish realm while we, down here on earth, hope he may soon land again on the progressive side of the barricade. There is still Gunter Grass and Garcia Marquez. Pinter, Lessing, Dario Fo, Habila, Ngugi.

But there was also an acute lack of young writers, angry and daring, determined to change the world and to offer new alternatives to the stale intellectual swamp created by the fundamentalism of finance and commerce, including its faithful servant – the thought-destroying entertainment industry that had lately swallowed almost all major publishing houses and independent bookstores.

It was easy and correct to a certain degree to say that it was now almost impossible to write a great novel against the establishment, if expecting it to be published and promoted.

Big media and publishing houses were far from independent. Most were part of large companies that would hardly be ecstatic to print books dangerous to their own interests and designs.

But the process of writing should never be fully influenced by mercantile considerations. A writer is a storyteller, an artist, a witness, a judge, and a thinker. He or she leaves important testimony about a particular time and puts on record what others often do not dare say. Financial reward is important (as reward for any difficult work should be), but longing for it can never influence the choice of the subject or the style in which the book is written. Otherwise, the result would almost certainly be rubbish.

I believed that the novel was the most complete artistic form capable of describing reality, the state of the world, the grievances and hopes of the people. I also believed that it should never aim at anything less than that.

I had attempted to write novels that showed the world through the eyes of war correspondents, visiting places that were rarely covered by the mainstream media, offering provocative points of view that were hardly acceptable to the entertainment business which now included most of the mainstream publishing houses. And writing itself, writing the truth was a privilege and joy. It was worth any inconvenience, any hardship.

It seemed that Arundhati Roy agreed with such views. So, was that it? Had a powerful history of literature ended? Had vital novelists become an endangered, almost extinct species? Were many of the most serious topics to be openly ridiculed forever, described as outdated and non-aesthetic, even anti-aesthetic? Would readers accept the results? For how long? Were novelists wholly expected to become entertainers, clowns, even liars? Were we supposed to forget so many great novels past?

Or were we going to swim with all our strength against the powerful forces crushing humanity?

I did not think we had much choice. At least, I did not. If we floated, if we allowed ourselves to be carried by the current, we would wash up on a land of irrelevance, oblivion, and shame.

I checked the screen. We were flying over Halifax. Moretti snored in his chair. His face appeared content.

I woke him and told him about the Italian countess who would join us in Todos los Santos.

"All right," said Moretti. "How old is she?"

"She claims she is around forty and looks fantastic."

"Tell me more."

"I don't know much," I said. "Right wing, probably fascist. Widow. Takes young lovers. She runs a shelter for homeless cats. Born and living in Venice."

"Conti!" howled Moretti. "I'll be damned! Francesca Conti. You are going to fuck Francesca Conti!"

"Is that good or bad?"

"Oh!" Moretti undid his seatbelt and bounced in his seat. "Good. Very good. Unbelievable. Can I watch? May I bring you fresh towels and Champagne?"

"Stop it," I laughed.

"Look," said Moretti. "I hope you've broken up with Reiko. Conti is not only a vamp, she's a vampire. A vampiress. She'll suck everything out of you. She is an absolutely disgusting human being – she is a fascist – she is worst than a fascist. Her ideas make the Northern League and Berlusconi look like Communists. She is beautiful. You must never meet Francesca Conti...or you must forget about all other women in the world..."

"Gino," I said. "I'm not fucking her. I can't fuck Fascists."

"What's wrong with that? Do not politicize sex."

"You want her, you take her. I'm tired of all that."

"Of all what?" Moretti screamed in disbelief. "This is what war correspondents do. We are expected to do it. At *least* that. Most of the men in this bloody world sit in their barracks, their dull housing, biting their nails, masturbating, dreaming about a tiny fraction of what we really do."

"Gino," I said. "Stop the myth. Not everyone is a sexual athlete..."

"Fine," said Moretti. "Are you taking Conti or not?"

"I'm not taking anyone. She kept insisting that she wants to see a war zone so let's take her into one. And she can screw you, or she can screw the entire leadership of the ENLP, I could not care less."

"National Liberation Front," corrected Gino.

"Whatever."

"All right," said Moretti. "All right, forget it. Is it Reiko?"

"Hell, yes."

"Karel," he said. "She is probably doing it with her husband right now. Marital duty, you know."

"Maybe," I said, opening again an outrageously boring *London Review of Books*. I wanted to go to sleep in a bed. I wanted to take a long hot shower, for an entire hour, and then pass out. That's all I wanted – nothing else.

We took an old jet to the capital and then a small turboprop to Todos los Santos.

The airport was deluged by military and transport planes. We passed through rigorous security checks before being allowed to leave the terminal.

Two local reporters were waiting for us. They drove us to the center of the city where the streets were empty. Sporadic exchanges of fire. Garbage covered the sidewalks. Most of the stores were closed. Anti-government and anti-American graffiti decorated the walls next to major intersections. Tanks were parked on two avenues in the center. Soldiers held machineguns ready, pointed straight ahead. Hardly anyone walked around and those who did kept their heads down, looking at their feet.

We were driven to the best hotel in town, *Posada de Virey,* obviously a gathering place of several government agencies from the United States. Two armored vehicles guarded the elaborate, pseudo-colonial entrance.

Gino checked in. A uniformed receptionist informed me in a ceremonious tone of voice that Her Highness Countess Francesca Conti was waiting for me in her suite.

"I would like to have my own room," I told her.

"Not a chance, sir. The hotel is overbooked with foreign aid agencies and with the press. We also have several friends from the United States staying here. But if you insist, you may share the room with Mr. Moretti."

"I'm not sleeping with you," said Gino. "You are hairy, you have a beard, and what's much worse, you are a man."

37

I entered the suite. The door was unlocked. The countess was sitting at a carved wooden colonial table, in an old chair, reading a book.

"Francesca?" I said.

"Well, yes," she turned toward me.

We studied each other for a long time. In that one moment I understood exactly what Moretti had meant. She was not beautiful, not in a classic sense, definitely not perfect, but her sexuality filled the entire room, her sexuality and her arrogant, self-assured presence. She was decked out in clothes that nobody wore anymore, other than at very closed and posh dinner parties in Europe. A long black designer skirt, black pantyhose and narrow low heeled shoes...a silk blouse and silk scarf. Her nails were perfectly groomed, long, dark red-brown. Expensive, discrete jewelry and a golden watch, perfectly applied make-up. Her face was long and narrow and with small features reminding me of a fox. Her brown hair fell naturally onto her shoulders. Her body was curvy with wide hips and artistically shaped calves, a long neck, thin waist, and narrow shoulders.

"All right," she said. "I expected you.... I thought you would be dirtier. Dust covered, smelly, straight from the battlefield."

I waved my hand toward her. "Are we going to a ball tonight?"

"Hell, no," she said. "Just the two of us, together, as we agreed. I hope you are not disappointed."

I was not disappointed. She looked exactly like the stereotype of a Northern Italian overdressed upper class slut. The "swept away" type. All that was missing was Giancarlo Giannini.

I did not feel at ease. A nice dinner first, a couple of drinks, then a short walk through colonial streets would have certainly smoothed our encounter. But the colonial streets were full of tanks and soldiers. The whole country was on the verge of civil war. And it appeared that she did not care about dinner or a walk. She had come for another very particular set of reasons.

"Do you like me?" she asked, straightforward. "Do you like your aristocratic whore?"

"Yes, I'm overjoyed by my aristocratic whore." I hung my clothes in an enormous walk-in closet. My voice did not sound natural and it wasn't.

"Take her, then," she said.

Reiko was gone, back in Tokyo. She had never asked me to stay. She had promised nothing. We had no future together – our future was a figment, a mere wish in my mind – it existed only in the imagination. Todos los Santos was real, the tanks were real, the countess was real. No matter how much I disliked reality, it was all that was available to me at this moment.

She crossed her legs. Silk stockings, of course. Dark. Heels, not too high, perfect. Probably no panties underneath.

"I hope you hate me," she said.

I had no strength left to hate. I felt jet-lagged, thoroughly exhausted. I was wondering how I could ever have said yes to her proposal to come to Todos los Santos.

After hanging my clothes I came closer to her, extended my hand and slowly caressed her hair and her face. I needed warmth, at least for a moment. An illusion of warmth. Not much, some.

"Are you insane?" she pushed my hand away. "I don't need any of this pre-pubertal stuff. I can get that in Venice. I need the real thing. Humiliate me, do something natural, damn it."

I needed to take a shower, desperately. I needed to sleep for at least twelve hours.

I dropped onto the soft comfortable sofa.

"Great," she said. "Did you come already simply by touching my neck."

"Fuck you, Francesca Conti," I said.

"I wish you could," she said.

She was laughing at me, straight at my face. I would have loved to have kicked her out, thrown her from the window, pushed her down the stairs, but this happened to be her room and the hotel was full.

"You left wing assholes have lately all been acting like pussies," she said, fixing her hair. "You can't even kick my ass!"

I was getting there. She was capable of making me mad, this Mussolini's brat.

"You are no different than all those European Union faggots."

The goddamned European Union. This managed to ignite me. I pushed up from the sofa and went straight at her. She would not shut up. I did what she was asking for. I kicked her ass. I kicked it with all my force, while she was sitting on the edge of the chair. She fell on the carpet. I kicked her ass again. She needed Giannini and I was going to give him to her. Another kick to punish her for all the goddamned cuts to social services for Italian workers and for kicking out illegal immigrants out of Europe. She howled.

"You swine!" she screamed. "More, now. Don't be a pussy."

I ripped off her skirt, I ripped off her pantyhose from the middle, from the crotch, and bent her over the cosmetic table in the corner of the room. My assessment had been correct: no panties. So be it.

"You dog!" she yelled. "You piece of Commie shit!"

I entered her from behind, not playing around, quite direct. I slapped her buttocks and inserted my thumb into her ass, all the way.

"*Que Cazzo*!" she whined. "You brutal animal! Cuban garbage!"

If I'd had my choice, I would have been far away, in another land, with a fresh breeze and soft sand and warm waves, but instead I was here, riding this Fascist brat, watching the reflection of her open mouth and pierced green eyes in the mirror, thinking that if this was going to be my last night, so be it, why not, damn it, and as I fucked her I felt angry, increasingly so. Not only was I totally pissed off, I felt sorry for myself.

We both collapsed on the carpet, without embracing, of course, without saying a single word for a long time.

"It felt great," she finally whispered.

She touched my arm.

"Thank you," she said. "And, I'm sorry."

"Sorry?"

"It was another woman, wasn't it? Another woman whose hair you were touching before."

Of course it was.

"Cut the crap, Francesca Conti," I told her. "It doesn't matter. Nothing matters. Only what's happening now. Always now..."

She stretched like a cat.

"Well," she said.

"Well..."

She kissed me on the cheek. "Nice meeting you, Karel."

"Okay. Same here," I said.

She got to her feet. She managed to do it elegantly even without her skirt, even with the ripped apart pantyhose.

She had plenty of style, I had to admit.

"Karel?"

"Yes, Countess?"

"Dearest, how are you going to introduce me to your repulsive, decadent Commie friends?"

I had not thought about this before but it was a legitimate question.

"I will present you..." I thought, "I will present you as 'The People's Countess.'"

"The People's Countess?" she laughed. "I hate people."

"I know," I said. "But you will have to pretend. Pretend that you love them. For at least one day."

"I'm not sure I can," she said.

She poured scotch from two little bottles from the minibar.

"Will we die tomorrow?"

"I don't know," I said. "I have no idea."

"Is it really going to be so bad?"

"Yes," I said. "It's going to be very bad and I don't think you should go anywhere. Stay in this room, order some drinks, and forget the whole thing."

"Oh no, I'm going," she said. "Such an *opportunity*. I flew twelve hours to see all this."

She was slurring "r."

"So it's really going to be bad?"

"I don't know," I said. "Probably."

She leaned over me and kissed me on the lips.

"Then fuck me once again, please."

38

I slept for some time, holding a pillow. Falling asleep had felt like a gentle descent, a smooth flight through white clouds. Sleep took me instantly away from the countess, from the obnoxiously posh hotel room in the middle of this miserable city, from a country on the brink of civil war.

My sleep destination however was equally disturbing. I went back in time, several years, to land on the deck of Pelni, an Indonesian ocean liner leaving Dili, East Timor. Almost dark. High waves sent foamy spray over the deck forcing me to constantly clean my glasses to retain sight.

A woman stared at me, standing motionless, close to the railing, while her husband washed his feet, preparing to enter a small Muslim prayer room. I studied her unable to determine where she was from.

I felt lucky to be alive, to be on this ship, taking me away from East Timor. I had seen enough, more than I had expected to see, and I felt exhausted, outraged, paralyzed. I tried to comprehend what I had witnessed. I needed to write its story, but my brain refused to function. I felt empty and sick. I carried several used rolls of film in my small equipment bag, two Leicas, five pairs of unwashed underwear, and not much more.

The woman wore a long Javanese dress, falling almost to her feet. Her fingers were long and slender. Ink-black hair covered her shoulders.

I had no idea why she looked at me with those huge black eyes. There was no smile on her lips, no expression of friendliness. It was as if she were waiting for something, as if she were trying to read something written on my face.

A few minutes later her husband went to pray. He said nothing to her. He left her standing on the deck, alone.

Almost immediately, she approached me.

"You saw...?"

"I don't understand," I said.

"You saw it?"

"Your husband is an official," I said. "He is from Java, isn't he?"

"Yes," she said. "Don't judge me, please. You don't know anything."

"Where are you from?"

"From here. From Dili."

"I enjoyed my visit very much," I said. "Wonderful place. Very beautiful scenery and friendly people."

"Stop it!" she screamed, but the sound of the waves muted her voice. "Don't torture me, please. You saw everything. You know..."

"What do you want from me?"

"Nothing. I want you to tell the truth. To say what you saw."

"Nobody cares," I said. "Nobody gives a damn."

"Nobody?"

"I don't know. A few people, maybe."

"But you care.... You came here," she whispered.

"Yes," I said. "But I hardly count. I go to many places. Nobody has any influence on me, and in turn, I have no influence on anybody."

"But you have to..."

"You speak good English," I said.

"Thank you. I studied English for years. I wanted to leave. But that doesn't matter. You saw..."

"They raped a whole village, from children to grandmothers. They carved obscenities into women's bodies, with the knives. They burned the clitoris with cigarette butts. They cut ears from several men. They killed others. For their own fun. To put some fun for them in the terror. Should I go on? It gets worse."

"I know all this," she said. "A third of East Timorese are dead. Since the invasion."

"That's about the correct estimate."

"They don't know it in Java."

"They don't?" I said. "They prefer not to know. Maybe they don't know anything about 1965 and about Aceh and Papua and who the hell knows what else."

"They pray," she nodded toward the room in which her husband disappeared. "They pray because they are scared. Because otherwise the whole nation would have to howl in the horror of its own guilt. They need it to be blasted loud, every day, the prayers, for hours, so they cannot hear their own hearts. They need it to overpower their conscience, even their consciousness. Their children are orphaned by the millions. Their children prostitute themselves and beg. Their cities are like purgatories, but they don't see it."

"They prefer not to see. They are deaf and mute in face of the bloodbaths and the misery of past and present." I nodded toward the prayer room. "He is going to come out, soon. He will not be happy to see you talking with me."

"Yes," she said. "I will find you later."

"It may not be wise."

"I have to."

She moved away. I sat on the bench, opened another pack of salty crackers. The bench would be my home for two days. The ship was sailing to Alor and than to Maumere in Flores. Government officials filled the private cabins. The alternative to the bench would have been an overcrowded, dark, communal room, packed with broken chairs, people, and plastic bags. I tried to enter one but was immediately repelled by a powerful stench. It smelled like the sprawling worst of modern Indonesia, full of unwashed bodies, repulsive spicy food, dirt, illness, and decay. I preferred to stay on deck, exposed to the strong wind and waves but also to fresh air.

A pack of salty crackers and five liters of bottled water would keep me company. And two packs of cigarettes in my bag.

The woman's husband appeared. He said nothing, nodded at her. She followed him upstairs, a few steps behind, to one of the cabins. She did not glance back at me.

As the lights from shore disappeared, total darkness gripped the ship, no stars and no moon. The waves increased in size. I felt tired and absolutely empty.

Someone vomited from the upper deck. Wind carried the puke so that parts of it hit my face. I poured water over my head.

People kept coming up to me.

“Hey mister! Where are you from? Hey, how much money you make? Where are you going? Indonesia, bagus!?”

“Bagus!” I would respond. Then puke from above hit my face again. Men laughed. They came to piss on the deck. The toilets had covered an entire floor below deck with urine and excrement up to their ankles. “Bagus!” I would repeat.

She came back around midnight.

“He is asleep,” she said. “I don’t have much time. He sometimes wakes up.”

I said nothing.

“Do you scorn me?”

“No,” I said. “For heaven’s sake, of course I don’t.”

“I scorn myself, sometimes. But most of the time I dream about being strong enough to kill him. It helps.”

“I understand,” I said. “How many years have you been married?”

“I don’t remember. I don’t want to remember. Five years, maybe. Or maybe longer. He took me when I was nineteen.”

“Took you?”

"Yes. One day I returned to East Timor from Bandung. I was studying there, at the university. I stayed in my house for two weeks. They raided our house, very late at night. They killed my older brother and they took away my sister. Then he came back, for me. He had his way with me for two days and three nights. He never shared me with the others. He did things to me, you know... I don't want to say it... Then he said I would soon marry him. I said I would kill myself but he replied that if I did, who knew what would happen to my mother and my younger brother."

"I'm sorry," I said.

"Then I had to convert. He took me to Java. I began to live with his family. He is hardly home. They torture me, you know... Not my body, but they do, in their own way. I have two children."

"Two children..." I repeated.

"I wish they would die," she said. "They are his children, not mine."

"Damn," I said. I gave her my card. "Run away," I told her.

"There is no place to run. This is Indonesia. If you run away and you cannot return to your own home, you end up a prostitute or a maid, or both. If you are lucky."

"I'll try," I said. "I will try to write, I promise. It's true that nobody cares, but I'll really try."

"Thank you," she said.

"I wish I could do more."

"You can't."

"Do you have a passport?"

"No. I have nothing. I'm his slave."

"Damn," I said. "I really hate this country."

"So do I," she said. "But I have never been anywhere else. Almost no one from here has been anywhere else. And those who travel are already programmed. They see but they pretend they don't see. They teach them how to be proud to be Indonesians. Instead of telling us how it is outside, they come back and say they are happy to be back in this country. We never learn anything from them. But I hope there is a world outside. And I hope I will see it one day. And I will never come back, no matter what. They killed so many people. There are so many people who are still alive but dead inside."

"You will see it. You will see the world outside," I said. "Though maybe it will not be as pretty as you imagine."

"It has to be better than this..."

"Yes," I said. "Almost anything is better."

"I knew it."

"And one day, your country will be free."

"I have almost nobody left, there. Please tell them, please tell the world outside what they have done to us."

"I will," I said. "I swear I will. I will always remember you."

I was exhausted after not sleeping for two nights. I wasn't sure what I was saying, but I kept speaking, anyway.

She made a cross with her fingers before leaving me. "May Jesus protect you," she said. I followed her with my eyes. I wasn't sure how much more of this I could take. She had passed her pain on to me, and now I had to carry it inside. I had to live with it for the rest of my life. I would live with her pain and with the pain of so many others.

I ran after her and stopped her. I took her hand. I pressed her forcefully against me. I felt every inch of her fragile body respond. I begged her silently for forgiveness. I was apologizing for my country which had allowed this to happen, and for everyone, and for all storytellers, including myself, who had failed her and failed countless of millions like her, all across the world.

39

Moretti came over to the suite at nine. “All set. They will enter the town center at eight in the morning, sharp. They will raise a red flag from the roof of the town hall, and later in the morning they will go back, behind the bridge. All this only if the army does not try to defend the city. The United Front believes that the army will not want to fight in the streets where it has no support. Both sides expect that there will be a battle in the vicinity of the bridge.”

He noticed the countess.

“*Francesca Conti, que piacere.*”

“*Ciao brutto,*” she smiled.

They shook hands.

“How many people will the United Front use?” I asked.

“Probably over 300 men and women. Maybe 350, but at most 400. That excludes indigenous farmers who have joined in the last few days.”

“What equipment do they have?”

“Most importantly, they have one anti-tank SPG-9, and one SA-7 Grail to take down a couple of Huey helicopters which the army will probably use. A few old machine guns.

Nothing else too impressive. As Felipe said, they really will use horses. That's for the ENLP. Other factions of the United Front of National Resistance have declared that they will intervene only if the forces of Felipe are almost wiped-out. The rest of the United Front has another 600 men in arms."

"Why don't they join from the beginning?"

"Because your friend Felipe is a jealous bastard. He doesn't want to share the glory," said Moretti. "Look, I'm kidding. The real reason is that he does not want the entire Front to disappear, in case something goes wrong."

"It seems that everything will go wrong," I said. "I don't know what he is thinking. There are at least five helicopters standing by right now, several tanks and at least one thousand government troops. Is he going to fight them with horses?"

"I'm afraid he will," said Moretti.

"Where are we going to be?" asked the countess.

"Right on the front line," I said. "Above the bridge. On the wrong side, from your political and geographical understanding."

"*Signora* Conti, with all my respect, seriously, you are not going," said Moretti. "You will have your fix of excitement right here, in Todos los Santos. You'll witness the guerrilla army taking this town. You'll see them hang the flag and hear them sing revolutionary songs. You will have enough stories for the rest of your life. Really, there is no reason to go to the river."

"Oh, I'm going," said the countess, smiling mischievously. "I didn't fly seven thousand miles to sit in this hotel."

Moretti shrugged his shoulders.

"I'll give them a donation," she said. "Ten thousand dollars, maybe, so they can drink themselves silly afterwards. Maybe more. I can easily give them enough to buy a tank. That's if they survive, of course."

"That's the people's countess!" I said. "That will definitely justify your presence. But tomorrow things could really get ugly. The front line between the two armies will be defined. Or maybe the entire ENLP will be wiped out. Gino and I will take no responsibility for your well-being. None."

"Very well," she said. "We will see."

"You will be on your own," I said. "We will get you there, but in the end you will be on your own."

"Fine," said the countess. "I'm always on my own. Except for my cats."

"Wear some sneakers or boots, at least," recommended Moretti.

"Are you insane?" She looked at him with profound scorn. "I'm a lady. I'll go there as a lady. Not as a tramp."

40

Reiko called my mobile phone at ten o'clock in the evening.

"Karel?"

"No," I said. "No. We really should not talk."

I cut the connection.

She called again, a minute later.

"Don't do this anymore, please. Talk to me..."

"It's not a good time, really," I said.

"Karel," she said. "I don't know how to say it. I swear, there was never a man I cared about more than..."

"It's too late," I said.

"No," she said. "It's not too late. It's never too late."

"Then say it!" I screamed. "What do you want to do? Not in one year, not in one month. Now! Do you understand? Now! What do you want to do now?"

"What do you want me to do? What should I say?" There was panic in her voice.

"I don't have any clue," I said. "It must come from you. I have no idea what you want to do. But if you don't know, we should not talk anymore."

"Never again?" she whispered.

"I don't know," I said. "I don't know anything, right now."

"How can you say this?" she asked.

The floor of the hotel shook as new troops moved through the city in heavily armored vehicles. After regrouping at the outskirts, these reinforcements would be sent almost immediately toward the river.

"What is that noise?" she asked.

"The army," I replied. "Tanks. It seems the government is moving an entire army into this bloody town."

"Does it have to be now? Do I have to decide what to do right now?"

"Yes," I said.

"Do you really expect me to drop everything this moment? Do you want me to change my life entirely? Do you want me to leave Tokyo, to leave my family and come to you?" I could hardly hear her voice. The windows rattled nonstop and the furniture clattered in the room. An ashtray walked to the edge of the table, flipped onto the ceramic floor, and broke into pieces.

"It's up to you," I said. "I can't tell you. I don't know myself."

She did not say anything for a while.

"I don't know, either," she said. "I swear, I wish I knew what to do, but I really do not."

We remained silent for several seconds. The feeling of exhaustion returned. I could not afford to feel down and out.

"I'm sorry," I said. "There may be no solution." We hung up.

Here in the suite, the countess slept on the bed. Moretti had dozed off on the couch. Maps, cameras, notebooks, film, and papers were spread all over. The movement of soldiers had stopped. A deadly silence hung behind the windows, not a single sound coming from the street.

I turned on the television. The US Secretary of State was denouncing Felipe's rebels, accusing them of taking advantage of the situation. According to the Secretary, the recent massacres around Todos los Santos were very sad and disturbing, but it was definitely not certain whether they had been performed by the paramilitary or by the rebels themselves. The United States stood firmly behind the present democratic government. The US stance was that the present conflict had its roots in poverty and that poverty could be eliminated only through the implementation of free market economic reforms, through foreign investment, and by the imposition of law and order in the country.

The famous writer who had recently denounced the government had been arrested.

The stock market had collapsed, the local currency had been devalued more than eighty percent in one day. The banks had frozen all savings accounts. Rich families were leaving the country by air, sea, and highway.

I went to bed where it took two hours to fall asleep. I kept the mobile phone on but Reiko never called again.

41

Early in the morning we dictated our first report to a stenographer at *The Weekly Globe* while Sub-Sub Comandante Felipe fought his way to the center of the city. Despite sporadic gunfire in the streets of Todos los Santos, the regular army refused to engage the ENLP here in a city now openly hostile to the government. Military intelligence obviously knew that the guerrillas planned to withdraw before noon. The government tanks pulled back to the barracks. The military waited.

Felipe rode his horse, his face covered by a mask, a red banner attached to the saddle and waving in the wind. A huge crowd of bystanders cheered his arrival. The main municipal building fell without a single shot. The mayor had fled long before the arrival of the ENLP, taking with him all his staff and his much hated fat German Shepard. Garbage of the previous days' fighting and demonstrations littered the streets of Todos los Santos. Barricades stood at several corners of the city center.

"This town is liberated!" shouted Felipe from the balcony. A crowd of some four thousand people cheered. The guerrillas fired a few shots into the air. Frightened pigeons took off toward the cloudy sky and disappeared behind the roofs.

What followed was the usual bravado of macho talk and cheers from the crowd and more shots and a few old Cuban and Nicaraguan revolutionary songs.

Moretti and I took photographs of bearded men and suntanned women on horses. We recorded the speech by Comandante Felipe and filed a second part of the report.

Apart from the center, the city remained unusually quiet.

Felipe spoke about the proletariat and the peasants, about the abuse suffered by the indigenous people, about the recent massacres by the paramilitary financed from abroad. He said there was no going back. The people had to defend themselves without counting on the corrupt police, the US-backed government, and the fascist army. The wealthy were exploiting the country, selling it for a pittance to foreign multinational companies. Seventy percent of the population was dirt poor, twenty percent illiterate. Money from the enormous natural resources of the land was disappearing into the pockets of business elites and corrupt government officials, and the rest went abroad – to so-called investors. The mounting foreign debt was to be paid from the pockets of the poor and the shrinking middle-class, while the rich stored the loot in foreign bank accounts, enjoying obnoxiously lavish lifestyles unthinkable even in the times of the colonial era. Social services for the majority had simply collapsed. Schools, hospitals, and roads were underfunded. Corruption flourished in all sectors of society. Those who had chosen to speak openly about the situation were intimidated, arrested, tortured, disappeared, or simply murdered.

While Felipe spoke, a few boys played with a soccer ball. Four local prostitutes dressed in their Sunday best and went to the square to show their support for the revolution. They balanced themselves on high heels and waved small red banners.

The countess was bored. Earlier in the morning she had eaten ice cream purchased from a street vendor that upset her stomach. She walked around the main square, mumbling something about the vulgarity of Spanish Colonial architecture. When she bumped into Moretti, she commented dryly: "This shitty event looks like a May Day celebration in Mestre, wouldn't you say, Gino? When are they going to bring a firing squad and execute someone?"

Two combat helicopters flew in at low altitude, almost touching the colonial roofs of the city, but no shots were fired.

Moretti and I interviewed two young fighters who only said that injustice would soon be eradicated. They promised that the proletariat, peasants, and intellectuals would soon be united, take over the entire city of Todos los Santos and, thereafter, the entire country, then all of Latin America, and the world.

A few teenage girls came to their rescue, stood in front of our cameras, clenched their fists and shouted: "Land to the peasants. Down with the *latifundista* dogs!"

After two hours there was nothing left to cover.

Churches rang their bells, a few more songs were sung, and the crowd broke into one of the liquor stores. There were no trials, no executions, no permanent arrangements.

Felipe gave his final speech which ended with the words: "There is nothing to celebrate, yet. We came here to demonstrate our strength, to give all of you hope and courage. Very soon, real fighting will begin. All those who are determined to fight this inhuman system are welcome to join us on the other side of the river. The military is much better armed, but it cannot annihilate our entire nation. One way or another, sooner or later, victory will be ours!"

Well before noon, the men and women of Sub-Sub Comandante Felipe started their slow withdrawal toward the bridge.

The three of us went back to the hotel, drank fresh squeezed lime juice and waited for the guide.

As agreed, the old man, Felipe's messenger, arrived at exactly 12:30. "Time to go," he said.

We walked two miles to the bridge, the countess balancing herself on shoes designed for Italian marble sidewalks, perspiring, probably damning herself and us and the entire revolution. Moretti and I dragged heavy equipment bags on our shoulders, sweating in the tropical heat.

We passed two army check points but they let us go through after studying our press credentials.

There was nobody on the bridge and it took us only a couple minutes to cross. On the other side, at an ENLP checkpoint, the old man uttered a few words and we were let through. Dozens of reporters waited in line, unsuccessfully waiving their press cards. Felipe had kept his word. It was obvious we were being given exclusivity.

We started climbing the hill and halfway up we found them: about four hundred men and women of the ENLP and a few dozen peasants, almost all carrying old rifles and AK-47s, ammunition belts around their waists, digging trenches or awaiting orders.

We photographed the people and the moment, while the countess studied their faces and bodies, and purred with satisfaction, sipping diet Coke from a can. This was what she had come for – the real battlefield, the real revolution – real war tourism.

Nobody spoke. Birds sang in the trees above us. The calming sounds of clear and pure water merrily jumped over boulders in the river below.

Felipe stood like a modern day Pancho Villa, massive beard and mustache, mask off, hat on, belts of ammunition around his chest and impressive belly. We ran our recorders:

"Are you sure you're not making a mistake?" I asked him. "Are you sure it's not too early for the real confrontation with the army?"

"I don't know," he said.

It seemed to me that nobody knew anything, lately.

"The thing is that there are several villages behind us. And they will take them if we do not draw the line right here. And we all know what happens when they take over a village."

"Are you going to talk to the government about the possibility of creating a demilitarized zone?" asked Moretti.

"We will. But first we have to hold the line. They will never talk unless they have no choice."

"What is your objective for today?" I asked.

"To hold the bridge," said the comandante.

"The bridge?"

"The line," he corrected himself. "We simply cannot let them pass beyond this point."

"No going back?"

"Not anymore," he said.

He barked orders and work accelerated. Trenches were almost finished and camouflaged. Moretti and I took shovels and dug our own holes, not far from the one of Felipe.

We were informed that there was an enormous amount of explosives attached to the bottom of the bridge. Several sets of wires had been dragged up the hill, ending in four different locations.

"Just in case," said Felipe.

The two geographical extremes of this provisional fortification were equipped with radio telephones connected to the trench of commanders.

The horses were left behind, three hundred meters away, on the other side of the hill where ammunition and rifles were stored in reserve.

An anti-aircraft SA-7 “Grail” was positioned at the right side, almost at the extreme end, while two SPG-9, 73 mm anti-tank guns controlled the road and the bridge from the left.

“Looks good,” I said to cheer up everybody.

“Bullshit,” said Felipe. “Not good. Not good at all, Karlito.”

“All right,” I said. “What do you want to hear, the truth? That I’m shitting in my pants by imagining what will happen to your people when they send two combat helicopters this way?”

“Sounds better, Karlito.”

I did not like any of it, really. And by the expression on Moretti’s face, I could see that he liked it even less.

“Anything you can think of?” asked Felipe. “You two cover wars all over the world. We are fighting only this one.”

“He wants us to get involved,” laughed Gino.

“Unethical,” I winked.

“You are involved,” concluded Felipe. “Why do you think I invited you here? To take my photograph?”

“I think you should keep at least twenty men behind, on the other side of the hill,” I said.

"Fifty," said Moretti.

"Nothing can prevent them from crossing the river somewhere else and attacking you from the back."

"I don't think they will do it. They will attack here," said Felipe.

"They have about a thousand soldiers," I said. "Maybe more. They were moving equipment and men all night long. What on earth makes you think they will send all of them into a frontal attack? Even as we speak, they are probably marching on this side of the river, a few kilometers away."

"We cannot take fifty people from this position," said Felipe.

"Send at least twenty," I insisted. "Put them at the top of the hill. Not at the very top, but close to it, on the other side, so they can monitor and cover your back at the same time."

"All right, I'll send ten. That's all I can spare."

"And why have you prevented the rest of the United Front from joining you?"

"Political reasons," he explained.

"Political reasons my ass," said Gino. "How much do you care about politics in a situation like this?"

"They may eventually join," he said.

He shouted orders again and eight men and two women left their trench and ran toward the top of the hill, with shovels and arms and ammunition.

"Give them a radio phone," suggested Moretti.

"I don't have enough. I have only two spare phones," said Felipe.

"*Coño*, don't you see that you have to communicate with your back, not with your sides," shouted Moretti. "You can see your sides fairly well from here, can't you? But you cannot see anything that is behind your ass and behind that hill."

Moretti spoke Italian, using his hands as an important and persuasive instrument of communication.

"Forget it," said Felipe. "They are not going to come from behind."

I was getting the point. He really did not believe they would do it. He was convinced that the assault would come straight on, with tanks and helicopters first. He did not think that they would even bother to use tricks. Not worth the effort. Not worth using military strategy to wipe out a few hundred badly armed peasants and bearded guerrillas. I looked at Moretti and I was sure he was thinking the same.

Another thing I could not understand was the bridge itself. There was no reason to spare it. Why not blow it now, before tanks and troops could cross? I saw a gang of disappointed reporters who were not permitted to join us. They were on the bridge, walking back toward Todos los Santos. Then the military did not let them stay on their side, either.

"Felipe, what about the bridge? Why is it still there?"

He looked at me for a while, without answering.

"I like that bridge," he said, finally.

I wasn't sure I had heard him right.

"You said you like that bridge?"

"That's exactly what I said."

Moretti stood there, his lower jaw dropping.

"What you are actually saying is that you have an emotional attachment to this bridge, right?" I was having second thoughts about staying there. *If he answers, yes, then the most logical thing would be to get out of there as fast as possible. Now, before it was too late.*

"You see, I grew up a five minute walk from here. I used to play on this bridge when I was a boy."

"And that is why you don't want it to be destroyed?" I said, with some desperation.

"Right."

"You really believe it will be standing there in twenty-four hours after the military attacks your position?"

"I don't know," he said.

"And we will all die defending this bridge of yours, right?"

"No, look..."

"Will we?"

He hesitated for some time.

"Maybe," he said, his voice suddenly harsh and determined. "But then, one has to die anyway. For something or for nothing."

I went to my trench. I went to my hole. Suddenly, I had no idea what I was doing here.

Everyone had lost it.

Carlos drove himself into a wall.

An Italian aristocrat dreamed of being sodomized by guerrilla soldiers.

Moretti simply didn't give a shit about anything.

Reiko was emotionally paralyzed.

And here I was, sitting in a trench, waiting to be blown sky high by a missile or mortar in a totally defenseless fortification outside some godforsaken jungle town scarcely visible on a map.

And right next to me, was the commander of the guerrilla army, ready to die defending a bridge because it was where he had played as a child.

I changed film in my cameras and dialed *The Weekly Globe* on my mobile.

"Green," I said. "Now shut up and listen carefully, ok?"

"All right," said Green. "What's going on? Are they attacking already?"

"Not yet," I said. "But just listen. Please."

"Go ahead."

"It doesn't look good. We may all get fucked today. If Moretti and I don't make it, you need to run the story as follows: '*There are approximately 400 men and women from the ENLP buried in trenches on the hill overlooking the river. They are very close to the bridge that connects Todos los Santos to the jungle villages. The ENLP is here to defend the villagers that would otherwise be massacred by the paramilitary and the army.*' Got it? No matter what you hear later, no matter what you read about the defense of the bridge, disregard it. The bridge is secondary. There are only two of us here –

Moretti and me. Only two witnesses. Nobody else except us knows anything. And this is our message and this is the point of the story: the ENLP is fighting for the villagers, not for the bridge. Repeat it, please."

I had to do it. I did not give a damn about what Comandante Felipe was defending. Four hundred men and women from the ENLP were here to defend the indigenous people behind our asses. That was what really mattered.

"Got it. Don't take me for a total idiot."

There was movement on the road, across the bridge. The army inching toward us.

"Karel," said Green. "Now you listen. I'm still your boss, am I not? Although you don't like that word, and I can't stand it either."

"Right."

"Listen. You and Moretti get out of there. Now!"

"No," I said.

"It's an order, damn it. I'm asking you and ordering you: get out of there. I checked on the situation. I contacted sources at the State Department. The US instructed them to finish the entire guerilla movement today. I was about going to call you. It's over. The revolution is over. They will slaughter everybody there. No fighting, no glorious battle. The military will use all its might. Nobody will come out of it alive."

"You know this is an exclusive cover story," I said.

"I don't give a fuck if it is a cover story!" Green barked. "I want both of you out of there. What's going on with you? Are you insane? Boys – I mean – fuck! I don't understand what happened to both of you. This is goddamn work, goddamn journalism. It's not worth it, don't you get it? Not worth fucking yourself for. You are my friends. Did I not explain this to you in New York? They do not care: our readers. They don't give a shit if they learn the truth or not. They don't give a damn if you live or die. And if you die, for them it will be another titillating story, don't you get it? Something to chat about. Or not even that! Nobody, nobody – listen carefully – nobody gives a shit what any reporter does. Nobody cares a fuck about anything. I want you and Moretti back here in New York, goddamn it. Now!"

"I don't think we can physically leave, anymore," I said.

"Wave a white flag, tell them you are having a heart attack, just leave. Tell that walking suicide Felipe that something terrible happened to your family all of a sudden. Lie. Get out of there!"

"Green..."

"No! Listen, I'll call the State Department. I'll call the embassy. I'll tell them to hold fire, to wait until you cross the bridge."

"Are they really controlling the whole show?"

"Of *course*. What are you thinking? You are standing on the American continent. North, South, Central, it doesn't matter. Nobody in the Americas can even fart without our blessing. You write about it yourself, why are you surprised now? Are you out of your five senses?"

"There's really nothing we can do at this point."

"You're insane," concluded Green.

"Would they really hold fire for the two of us? Two critical reporters. Two *anyone*?"

"Of course they would! You're an American. Gino is Italian. Stop asking stupid questions. You're white, damn it! It all comes down to that. They don't give a shit how many indigenous, Asian, or African people get slaughtered. Two thousand, two million, they don't give a fuck. They think they don't count. There's too many of them, they have no feelings, no brain. *That's* how they think. Wake up! I'm going to call them. I'm going to get you out of there."

"Don't!" I shouted. "We're not going anywhere. Somebody has to cover this. Green, they are going to massacre everybody in the jungle."

"Of course they will!"

"Doesn't anyone care?"

"I do. You do. Amnesty International cares. That's about it. Who gave a fuck about the Indonesians butchering the East Timorese? Who cares what happens to the Papuans? Who cared about how many millions we killed in Indo-China? Who cared about the millions of people dying from AIDS? Who cares about half of the population of this planet living in the gutter? Why on earth should anyone care now about Todos los Fucking Santos?"

"I rest my case," I said. "Anyway, we're not leaving."

"Your wife called again. She keeps calling *The Globe* every ten minutes. She is heading your way. To Todos los Santos. Do you see, now?"

"Green," I said. "I don't have a wife. Since when do I have a wife?"

"Reiko. That Japanese girl. She said she is your wife."

"She did?"

"Yes, of course. Are you insane? Are you and Moretti drunk? Do you even remember who your mother is?"

"Not going there," I said. "All right, what did she say?"

"She is at the airport somewhere in Japan. She is taking the first available flight to San Francisco and from there to Mexico City and to Todos los Santos. She threw a fit when I described the situation. I told her everything I'm explaining to you now. She screamed at me. She said that all we want is blood. She said she left everything behind, that all she wants is for me to get you out of there. She said she'll burn down our bloody magazine. I've never heard a Japanese woman screaming and using such foul language. Did you teach her?"

"Green," I said, while I watched at least a hundred men approach the river. "It's too late. We wouldn't be able to get out of here."

"Are you sure?"

"Yes."

"Goddamn it!"

"Right," I said. I pinned the phone between my ear and shoulder, zooming at the soldiers, taking the first photographs.

"What should I tell her?"

"Tell her, thank you," I said. "Just thank you."

"That's it?"

"That's it," I said. "But don't forget."

"Thank you for what?"

"She will know," I said.

"Fine. I'm sending Joanne and Hide as back-up. Immediately."

"Good. Don't forget the bridge. Don't mention the bridge anywhere. It's the villages behind our asses."

"As you say."

"They're coming."

"Time?"

"14:28, local. One hundred men of the regular army. No equipment, no vehicles so far. Green, I have to go, to save batteries. I'll call."

"Fuck," said Green. I cut off the connection.

I ran to the next trench and found Gino. I told him about Green's information. He looked at me in disbelief.

"You didn't know?"

"Didn't know what?"

"All of that. Where have you been?"

"In Bali," I said.

"I thought that when we spoke on the plane..."

"What are you telling me, Gino?"

"I thought you'd had enough of all this."

"Enough of what, damn it?"

"Enough of everything," he spread his arms wide. "I thought that you knew that this will be it. The endgame. I thought Conti was part of your endgame. I thought you wanted to go out in style."

I looked at him, his face calm and remote.

"You can still probably get out of this," he said.

"You're insane," I told him.

"Yes," he answered. "Don't you know? Everybody on this hill is insane, one way or another. Mostly another."

42

There was no warning. Two Huey Cobra helicopters stormed the horizon, flying in close formation, side-by-side, toward the hill.

Four missiles separated from the gunship and cruised our way. I caught it on film and then fell to the bottom of the hole.

Guns barked almost simultaneously, and soon every other sound, and every sense, was overwhelmed by a deafening explosion. Probably four explosions but in a single eruption, shaking the ground. Earth fell on my body from all sides. I was not wearing a helmet. The dirt poured over me like water.

I looked outside. Government soldiers were crossing the bridge, running in broken ranks.

Sounds of shooting everywhere: from our side, from across the river, from the bridge itself. I worried about the dirt on my lenses, cameras.

The *Federales* had not brought artillery and I wondered why.

Somebody was screaming, not far from me, but I could not see anything from where I was.

The helicopters returned again. An anti-aircraft missile flew from the right side of the hill. A few moments later there was an explosion and black smoke from the back of the helicopter and it started to spin, looped totally out of control. I took pictures before it crashed into the trees of the jungle not far from where we were. There was a tremendous explosion and a tower of smoke shot straight up to the sky. There were cheers but not for long. Soon all human sounds were muted by greater roars.

Our position came under constant fire from approaching tanks, which remained out of range of Felipe's SPG-9s.

Moretti moved to my trench, two cameras hanging from his neck.

"Should we go?" I asked.

We crawled toward the center, where Felipe and his closest men, as well as the people's countess, were positioned. Along the way we saw men and women shooting from old rifles and AK-47s. Some were already dead and many were injured.

The countess was pale and her lips were shaking.

"I have to go," she repeated very quickly. "I have to leave, boys, I have to go right now."

"There is no place to go," said Moretti. "There are no escape routes."

The helicopters returned. A pair, again. The military – plenty of reserves, obviously.

Four more tanks approached the bridge.

"Blow that shit!" Moretti yelled at Felipe, pointing at the bridge, but the comandante pretended not to hear him. He was smoking his fat *puro*, his fists clenched, eyes shining. He was mad, absolutely out of his mind, there could be no doubt.

All right, I hoped, maybe he is waiting for the tanks to come closer so the SPGs can be used. Unfortunately, the guerrillas had only two SPGs, old equipment, brought by "mules" – arms traffickers – after a strange deal with the disintegrating Soviet Army. It was not certain whether or not the SPGs would work at all and now the battlefield was imploding beneath the helicopters and as the tanks moved closer. I saw two ENLP fighters leaving their trenches, throwing Molotovs and other homemade junk at the tanks, then falling dead instantly under the fire of the approaching government soldiers.

Suddenly a recoilless anti-tank gun fired its 73 mm projectiles. Amazingly, it worked. The first tank caught fire, stopped, blocking the way for the entire column. Cheers rose around us, but there was not much to celebrate, it seemed to me, not much at all, because four new tanks took positions on the other side of the river and pointed their cannons straight at us.

Moretti chewed his lower lip then swore and clicked the shutter of his camera, swearing and clicking the shutter again and again and I did the same, automatically, until my finger grew numb.

There was booze available. We had brought plenty of it. Moretti was drinking something industrial imported from Moscow. I hit on warm vodka straight from the bottle. At first it made me sick but the second dose was no problem as always. There was no way one could stay sober and sane amid the calamity. The countess was now howling, a sound almost inhuman, as if she were a cornered wounded animal. Her clothes were wrecked, dirty, her elegant shoes missing. Tears cut through the dirt on her cheeks, streaked through her heavy make-up, like lava flowing through volcano ash.

The guerrillas' left wing was taking almost all the fire because it was closer to the road and the bridge. I assumed there was probably nobody left alive there or able to fight anymore. Then Felipe barked again, screamed something into his primitive radio phone, to send another forty men and women from right to left. Soon after I saw them crawling behind our trench. I wondered what would come next, whether the army would bring artillery after all and wipe us off the face of the earth or whether they would merely poison us with gas. At least the helicopters had stopped roaring in, probably because their soldiers were now too close to our positions. They were climbing the hill. Felipe's men threw hand grenades to prevent the soldiers from getting too close but they kept climbing and falling, some dead, some injured, a scene of real carnage, which I had not witnessed since Bosnia.

It all looked very different through the camera lens. In real life, shit flew every which way. Bullets whistled above your head or hit the soft brown terrain of the hill. Incoming mortars hissed and flew from across the river. Tanks blasted periodically at your positions. It seemed much slower if you zoomed in on it or even if you zoomed out as much as you could. Not that you were any safer looking through a lens. Focusing and narrowing what you saw could provide a momentary illusion of safety, but in reality you remained smack in the middle of the horror. There a man's body – smashed against the earth, covered by dust, exposed. Filming or photographing an event made you an observer – flattened the dimension of the experience even as you precisely captured a moment. Working the camera distanced your perspective as you worked, concentrated. But only for a time. Then you put down the camera and it was all terribly real. Extremely real – right there in your face more than a picture through an eyepiece now. The horror engulfed you in becoming multi-dimensional again, too real.

I dialed Green. I tried to give him an idea of what was going on. I checked my watch, surprised that it was already four in the afternoon. Green took notes, and then I disconnected the mobile immediately, unwilling to listen to anything, my interest in the outside world totally lost. It was important to cling to this hill, to this earth, that was all, a hill that was not even mine but which had been blasted into my body and which covered me from head to toe. This was a negligible stripe of land hardly visible from space but supremely significant to several hundred men and women fighting here, and dying, and to the billions of people in the world who had lost their voice, their hopes, and their ability to defend themselves.

Green called again. At first I could not hear him. Then the connection improved, and in between explosions I heard him shouting: “Hold on there, don’t give up! They took the Congress in the capital. The United Front took the Presidential palace! The UN Security Council is holding an emergency session, there may be a ceasefire at any moment…”

There was no sign of any ceasefire here. The army had not used a thousand soldiers, they had hardly used six hundred. They were trained and well fed and armed to the teeth. Most of the soldiers had crossed to our side of the river now, using the bridge and fighting for every inch of the slight strip of land between the hill and the river. The soldiers could not find much cover, so their best option was to move as quickly as possible forward. And move they did.

I saw fear on the faces of the ENLP fighters. I saw brutal injuries and dead bodies strewn on the hill. This hill of doom had become the last place anyone would want to be, but we all knew that it was long since no less deadly to flee than to fight. We had no choice. And we had chosen, long since.

Finally I realized what Felipe had planned. It was insane, inescapably, but somehow it made sense. He jerked the fuse and the bridge exploded, literally flew into the air, disconnecting our battlefield even farther from rest of the world. For several seconds, debris landed everywhere. Twisted metal punctured what had earlier been crystal-clear water, now muddy and running with dirt and blood and dead bodies.

The fight was now between only the ENLP and the regular army. Face to face. Felipe had *invited* the army across the bridge. The people's bridge. I caught a smile on Comandante's face – a horrific smile on his lips as his eyes watered, the rest of his face twisted in pain – this was what he had waited for. This was his grand plan. A dogfight on his side of the river, the people's side. An honest, man-to-man fight, with the guerrillas, dug in uphill.

I took photographs of what was left of the bridge and then of the tears on Felipe's cheeks.

The *Federales* were definitely better armed. And they had more men, but from now on they would be forced to fight from below.

Felipe would of course make the argument that the situation had improved. Strategically, it looked to me as fucked up as before. Or worse. While before there had been a slight chance that the army could have been worn down or slowed and been made wary of fighting at night, now they had to fight to the end. Their only escape route had been cut off.

Felipe shouted orders and almost all his men and women roared and yelled and jumped out of the trench, running and shooting downhill and Moretti and I went too, running after them. So much for being dug in. Felipe had turned everything around. He heaved out of the trench with his AK-47 hung on his shoulder, shouting obscenities, excoriating the mothers of the federal soldiers, all the while propelling his huge and fat body with unbelievable velocity down the hill.

Mortar flew over our heads and struck in a powerful explosion directly behind us, inside the trench we had abandoned.

We returned and there she was, the countess, lying on her back, looking up at us with her green eyes, her face as pale as toilet paper.

"What happened?" she asked.

It was dirty inside the trench. Only half of her body remained intact. The upper part. From the waist down it was just a dark mess of liquids, a thing hard to define. No legs. Definitely no legs.

"Nothing serious," I said, about to puke. "Does it hurt?"

"No," she said. "Not much. But I can't move. I don't think I can get up."

She was in shock. No pain, just numbness. I had seen this happen before, and I had never understood. Once, a doctor friend tried to explain, but I still did not get it.

"Take my picture, both of you. Maybe it will make it into the newspapers back home, so everyone can see how brave I was." She tried to smile. "Take my picture, please."

I looked at Moretti.

We took a few photographs each. She could hardly move her lips. Moretti swore.

Eventually we got into it – shooting an entire roll of film each.

The fighting was going on full force under the hill and then we heard shooting somewhere from above. We were in the middle of it.

"They are coming from the other side," screamed Moretti. "We told Felipe they would. Now they will all get fucked."

Indeed they were coming. The regular army. At least a hundred of them. They progressed slowly toward us. It was obvious they were very uncertain, not knowing how many of our men and women had survived or remained in the trenches.

"We have to go, Countess," said Moretti.

"Don't leave me here," she begged. "It's starting to hurt now. A little, but it hurts. I have no idea what's happening."

We could not even try to lift her up. There was no way of lifting her, of trying to carry her anywhere. Almost nothing remained of her down below – virtually nothing intact. There was no morphine around. We looked at each other, Moretti and I.

"I can't do it," I said.

Moretti took a revolver from the pile of arms left at the bottom of the trench. He stood there, with the weapon in his hand, unable to decide, an insane expression on his face.

By then she had lost too much blood. She died, before Gino had to fire. She did not make a sound. A long spasm went through her body, and her face regained serenity and a certain elegance, despite the brown mask of dirt covering part of it.

Moretti picked up two AK-47s. He handed me a Kalashnikov, dropping his cameras on the ground.

"Damn it, Moretti," I said. "It's against principle."

"There are no principles on this hill," he responded.

"We need to report," I said.

"We did. There is nothing to report anymore. Do you know how to use these things?"

We both did.

I closed my eyes for a few seconds.

"Keep the cameras," I said.

He hesitated for a moment, then picked one up again.

The machine gun felt heavy and clumsy. I inserted the magazine full of ammunition and felt it lock in.

"Fuck," I said.

Soldiers were heading our way. Not many. Twenty or thirty, slowly descending from the hill, with almost no cover, shooting into the air, as scared as anyone, as fucked as anyone – members of the regular army – boys taken by force from the shanty towns of the capital city. Gino and I crawled to the edge of the trench.

I had never excluded the possibility that this might one day happen. I'd had nightmares about it but now that it was here I almost felt relief.

"Fuck all, fuck the motherfuckers!" yelled Moretti.

Then he produced a deafening scream. Loud and horrible. He howled with a voice well trained during countless dark alcoholic orgies in Russia. He howled like a madman, and we both opened fire. I heard myself screaming too, obscenities in various languages. All I saw now were figures of approaching soldiers, some stopping, some stumbling uncertainly over rocks, one or two falling, the rest scrambling for cover behind scarce trees and rocks.

Moretti and I continued shooting and howling and probably shitting at the same time until there was nothing left in the entire universe, nothing except the two of us and our screams and the slight resistance of the smooth triggers of the machineguns.

As it turned out, the army had sent reinforcements to the river. The soldiers crossed on large rubber boats, half a kilometer downstream. Meanwhile, Felipe and his men were getting fucked royally as we had predicted, somewhere near the river. We were unable to see them, anymore. It was probably only the two of us holding this hill and we were also as good as dead, and I did not care about anything, could see no hope for getting out of alive. I wanted it to be over soon. I wanted to avoid a terrible injury, being hit in the face and surviving. I had seen it happen, the consequences. I had been horrified by the possibility of losing my face, my jaw, of waking up and realizing that I was disfigured forever. This fear never left me, no matter which war I covered. Only my face, I did not care about anything else. I only wanted to keep my face.

I could never describe the war. It was like this, absolutely nothing concrete, no heroes in sight, all shitting, howling, sweating, dirty, bleeding, screwed, mad, drunk.

Those few men at the top of the hill did not have grenades or they did not think about using them, because if they had, we would have been gone by now, wiped out.

We continued shooting and suddenly I saw Moretti get hit. His shirt was soaked with a dark red liquid. There was an explosion nearby and I felt pain in my left shoulder. A few moments later something hit me again, this time lower, on the side of my body. It hurt badly but was bearable.

We did not stop. We fired toward the top of the hill, unable to see much, anymore, unable to remember what we were doing here. Then I saw an enormous red flag on top of the hill and our howls met the howls of hundreds of other throats and I saw men in masks running down the hill, toward us, toward the river, I heard powerful explosions and shouts. A few moments later I felt the presence of dozens of men and strong hands lifting me from the ground and someone hugging me and I felt the beard of another man brushing my face and I saw my cameras on the shoulder of a guerrilla fighter, and I saw Moretti being carried somewhere, too, and a deep voice telling me: "It's all right. You did it, *'pañeros.* They did not pass, damn it! They did not pass, motherfuckers!" The guerrillas carried our bags and cameras and loaded us on their horses and I finally realized that the United Front had moved in, no matter the agreement with Felipe – they had finished the military on this side of the river, they had won the battle – and then I felt pain in my side and in my shoulder and total exhaustion and I could not speak or move. I had no desire to think and I closed my eyes, falling somewhere, deeper and deeper where I could not hear voices or sounds, where there was no movement, only tranquility, certainty, and calm.

43

When I opened my eyes, the first thing I saw was her face. Reiko sat next to my hammock, dressed in her city clothes.

She sighed with relief and came closer and kissed my face. She smelled like a great city, of sophisticated perfume and expensive clothes. And also of travel – of airports and cigarettes.

"How long was I out of it?" I asked.

"Almost two days," she said. "You lost blood and your wounds were infected. Now they say it should be all right."

She made an attempt to smile. It looked like a mask. She was exhausted.

"How is Gino?" I asked.

"Not good," she said. "But he should make it."

"And Felipe?"

"He's all right. A few scratches. He's boozing with your colleagues."

It was true. I heard the voices of Hide and of Joanne and Felipe nearby.

Reiko stared at me in disbelief. She tried to say something but her voice broke on the first syllable. She made another attempt.

"We are going home," she said.

"Home? There is no home." I wondered.

"There is," she said.

"Together?"

"Yes. Karel," she said very quietly.

I had no idea what she meant.

"What happened?" she asked. "You joined the revolution? You and Gino defended the bridge? You almost died. Was it worth it? Is any of this worth dying for?"

"I don't know," I said. "We had no time to think about it."

"You had your entire life to think about it. You had your entire life to think about."

"Probably so. It's definitely worth living for."

"I left my husband," she said. "I..."

She inhaled smoke, held it in, then exhaled with hardly a sound.

"I filed divorce papers. Keiko is with her grandparents. Is this what you wanted?"

"Yes," I answered, honestly.

"I'm not sure the two of us can make it.... There is nothing we have in common, there is hardly anything we can agree on."

"We can try," I said. "That's what we can do. We can try."

She squeezed my hand.

"You're insane," she said.

"That's true," I agreed. "But insanity is attractive And it's definitely contagious. There is very little more depressing than permanent calm."

The heat had become unbearable, even in the shade of the tent. Night approached. Singing washed from every corner of the camp. People celebrated. They danced. I felt pain that was not unbearable.

Hide and Joanne came over and shared the latest news. The capital city was firmly in the hands of the rebels. The wealthy continued to flee across the border, to join their fat bank accounts abroad. The local currency had collapsed. The United States had condemned the revolution, describing it as an undemocratic coup by those who wanted to reverse the course of history. The US called for the return of the former government. Thousands of American troops and military equipment were being flown to an adjacent country, while volunteers from Latin America and Europe, and even the US, had begun offering their lives to the revolution.

"If we have to fight the Yankees, we will," said Felipe.

This felt like revolutionary Nicaragua all over again. But the revolution in Nicaragua had failed, choked with the terror unleashed and funded by Washington DC. That revolution had been suffocated, raped, destroyed. I wasn't sure if Felipe's country had a chance, or if any country on earth had a chance to go its own way.

"You may end up like Indonesia, like Chile, or like Nicaragua," I told him.

"They cannot destroy the whole world, for their greed," said Felipe.

"They can," I said. "You know they can. They've managed to destroy more than half of it already."

"There's only 300 million of them."

"It's not only *them*," I said. "If it were only them, everything would be much easier. It's not only the United States, and you know it. It's business. Big business all over the world. These gangs own the world – millions of men and women who won't control their unbridled lust for making deals, for possessing more than the others, for seizing power and control over every god-forsaken corner of the globe."

"Unbridled lust is a mental state, an illness," replied Felipe. "We can't be the hostages of sick individuals, can we? We can't be their slaves forever. If they don't want to cure themselves, we have to fight them."

"They own the world," I said. "They own the media, public opinion, armies, factories, entire countries. They own the governments. They own everything."

"They don't own us," he said. "They don't own you or me, or any of my men and women. Therefore, they don't own everything! And they don't own millions, maybe billions of people like us in all corners of the world. As long as we hold out and fight back, there is at least some hope left."

I felt suddenly cold. I had a fever and my entire body began to shake. I squeezed Reiko's hand.

Felipe went off to sing outdated songs with Italian revolutionary tourists.

"Let's go home," I said.

"Soon," she whispered. "We'll go very soon. When you can walk."

44

They buried more than two hundred men and women from the United Front, all with military honors, and then they buried the countess, refusing requests for the transfer of her body made by her family and the Italian Embassy. "This is where she died, and this is where she will be buried," the spokesperson of the revolutionary government declared.

Felipe stood next to the deep hole into which her body would be lowered, wrapped in a red flag. Ten *guerrilleros* stood ready to shoot into the air. Then Felipe decided to give a speech. He held forth, drunk, sweating but determined.

"She was a whore," he started, moved by his own words, voice trembling. "She was a whore but she was our whore, the people's whore. No matter where she came from, no matter what her background was, she arrived here, to give support to the poor peasants of this tortured land. Even a whore is in her soul a mother, a sister...." He swallowed, heavily. "And she died because she loved our simple people and she wanted to be with them when they took up arms in defense of their rights and lives. She died for the revolution, not for that brothel – the old puppet state."

Reporters from all the major Italian newspapers, from all the major networks, from all over Europe and the world recorded the scene and speech.

"She died in a trench like a soldier, as one of us," he paused. "As a hero. And so did her countryman, the famous Italian journalist and philosopher and womanizer Gino Moretti...."

Somebody whispered in his ear.

"Damn, I'm sorry, Gino did not die! Gino fought and emerged from this fight alive, as did my brave friend Karel, an American hero, a true revolutionary and a great friend of this country!"

I saw my passport being revoked. I damned Felipe and his drunken stupor.

There was a salute and flashes went off, and the countess covered in a red flag was lowered to her last place of rest.

"No pasaran!" The Sub-Sub Comandante clenched his fist.

It seemed that there were hundreds of foreigners present. Intellectuals, writers, journalists, two Socialists from the European Parliament, even four Ambassadors from left-wing South American countries. Despite the funerals, the atmosphere seemed festive. I wondered where all these people would be when the first American bombs started falling on the capital city, when the blockade was applied, when food and medicine and consumer goods disappeared from the shelves.

I closed my eyes and paid my own silent tribute to Francesca Conti, the Italian countess who hated the poor. As despicable as she truly was, she never uttered a lie, she never faked pity, never pretended to be compassionate. She was probably the most honest person I had ever met in my entire life.

Photographs by Moretti and myself had been taken from the camp to the capital city while I was unconscious. *The Weekly Globe* offered us an enormous sum of money for the exclusivity, for the story of Francesca Conti, and for the story of the battle for Todos los Santos. It was more money than I had seen in my life: seven digits. I was told there was plenty of room for negotiation but I decided to accept the offered sum – I had no idea how to spend it, anyway.

Our photographs made the countess more famous than any member of royalty or aristocracy anywhere in the world. She became a cult figure, a reincarnation of royal bravery and decency. Gino and I supplied pictures and refused to write a text, allowing others to endlessly fill in the gaps with speculation, sentimental rubbish, and outright fantasies.

There were great demonstrations all over Europe, especially in Italy, in support of the United Front. The Countess Francesca Conti became the new symbol of the Italian left-wing, of new humanism. All over Capri and Rome street vendors sold T-shirts with insignias – "Francesca Conti – Italian heart" – in many world languages, even in Korean and

Swahili. A street in Milan was named after her. When one of her previous young lovers got drunk in Rome and claimed that her favorite saying was, "Fuck all poor bastards with a hot iron rod straight up their asses," he was chased by the mad crowd and forced to eat dog shit, in the middle of Via Veneto. A Roman daily loosely paraphrased Emanuel Kant by declaring: "From now on we should never judge a person by appearance. There are millions of secrets in the night sky above us. And there are millions of secrets inside us, in our human hearts."

After her death, the Italian state took over her shelter for homeless cats, by force of enormous pressure from the concerned public.

45

Reiko bent over me, her long black hair falling on my face.

"Do you like it here?" she asked.

"I never liked it more anywhere in the world," I said.

"Thank you," she said. "I told you there is a home for us. This house was empty for many years. My parents moved to the city, but they never thought about selling this place. I grew up here. I lived here when I was a little girl."

I liked the way her hair tickled my face. I closed my eyes again.

"I feel so relieved," she said.

"I want to stay here," I told her. "I don't want to go anywhere. Just live here with you."

"For a month?" she laughed.

"I don't know. I don't want to think about the future. I've never felt like this before."

"How?" she asked. "Content? Happy?"

"Yes. But more than that. I'm not sure. Really, it feels like coming home from a very long and turbulent journey."

"To me."

"To you."

There was a simple Japanese room with two futons pushed together, with a straw mat and two large windows facing the sea. The entire house was built of wood. There was a small garden outside, with sculpted trees and bushes. There was a narrow beach across the street. We could hear the sound of waves and the cries of seagulls. Once in a while, a man selling noodles went by with his cart. Every four hours, a ferry entered the port and announced its arrival with a long and melancholy siren.

"We are still young but there is so much to heal," she said.

"We will do it together."

"Always, everything?"

"Everything," I said. "I will learn your language."

"I speak yours," she said.

"No," I said. "It is not my language and it never was. I learned the language well, and I write books using it, but it's not my language."

"I understand," she said. "We will teach each other. I feel happy and it makes me almost frightened."

"Don't feel frightened. It's fine now. Everything is fine. Everything will be fine from now on."

But I knew what she meant because I felt the same – the feeling of happiness was almost painful. I watched her bare feet on the bamboo floor, her long fingers, her hair. My love for her hurt, somehow, and I did not understand why, but even this pain was good. I did not try to suppress it.

The world outside seemed suddenly unsettling. I felt no desire to be part of it. I wanted to stay here, in this peaceful town on the island whose name I could not even remember, lost somewhere between Shikoku and Honshu. The world outside had taken my parents away twenty years ago when I was least prepared, on the motorway between Prague and Moravia. Later, the world threw me into a whirlpool of wars and conflicts, suffering and hunger, lies and emptiness. For many years, I fought and rebelled, despising the way the world was arranged. I tried to expose injustice, to help those who were starving, to shame those who sacrificed the lives and well-being of millions of people for their own gain. I had no privacy, no personal life. And now I did not miss anything. The world had pushed Carlos to suicide. It had taken Ana and so many others. We had all fought and we had failed. There was no visible change for the better. I had seen it – all there was to see – I had witnessed birth and death, betrayals and incredible loyalty, fear and brutality, tenderness and compassion, but for now I felt full, I could not absorb more. I had no desire to see further. I had learned and understood many things. I had written books, but it had never been good enough because words could not express everything. There was a bitter limit to words.

This island and the woman who had brought me here – it was enough. It had to be enough, no matter her story, her past. I had no doubt about this. I had no doubts for the first time in my life. I wanted to forget everything, at least for now. I wanted to rest for days and months to come, to breathe fresh cold air from the sea, and to listen to the sound of the waves.

"You will help raise my daughter," she said.

"Yes," I said.

"We will have a child together. Maybe, one day."

"Yes," I said.

"We will put our pasts behind us."

"We will."

"I want to be yours," she said.

"And I belong to you," I answered.

I embraced her, and moved to take her completely but she gently resisted.

"No," she said. "Let's start from the beginning. Let's not rush things. We now have all the time there is, for ourselves. There was a boy and a girl and they lived in two far away places. In two different countries on two different continents. I want to hear your story, from the beginning. All about you. I want to hear everything about you, before things became the way they were when we first met. I will do the same. I will tell you all about me, about my first steps and my first dreams. I will tell you what I wanted to be and what I never became. All about myself, before things became confused. And we should stop there, where it all went wrong. And pick up the broken pieces, together. And start from the beginning, together. And learn how to walk again. And forget. Together. And forgive, together. And grow up and become adults, together. And then age together."

46

In those days we did not visit our neighbors. People in Reiko's town talked as they always talk in small provincial towns. They said Reiko had come back and brought with her a foreigner. They found out that she had left her work and her husband. They said we both came from a far away place, from a country where people fought for a different world. They said that we desperately needed rest and that Reiko and her man had now forgotten about the world around. Often walking at night to the shore and sitting by the old lighthouse, they resembled two ghosts more than two people in this world.

Heavy winds arrived. It rained for many days. Eventually the sky cleared, and at night we saw again thousands of distant stars shining from an unimaginable distance. Time passed fast, but we paid no attention to it. We slowly explored the island, its countless curves and hidden bays, hills with ancient temples, the forest with fresh water springs, paths that led nowhere and bridges connecting one dormant community with another.

September added fascinating colors to the surrounding hills.

Reiko's divorce papers arrived. We were married in a simple civil ceremony at the municipal building on the island.

Then one day, a neighbor boy knocked at our door. He was fifteen years old and his face looked confused and full of grief. He bowed, apologized for disturbing us, and expressed his condolences to me. Then he left. I had no idea what he was referring to. Reiko and I had been cut off from the world for weeks, maybe months.

Reiko turned on the dusty and unused television set in the corner of the living room. After several moments I understood. Repetitive footage showed large passenger jets ramming the two towers of the World Trade Center in New York. People raced away from the smoke and fire, in panic, expressions of fear and disbelief on their faces. Men and women jumped from the windows of the burning towers. And then the buildings, one after another, collapsed.

I was speechless, eyes glued to the monitor, smoking one cigarette after another. Reiko probably expected me to say something. Words would have felt too slight, almost meaningless.

"When I was young, I used to go there once a month," I said finally. "I used to take the elevator to the top floor and sit there, looking at the city and at the bay below me. I thought it was the most beautiful view in the world. I still think it is. I mean, was..."

Reiko said nothing. She looked stunned.

I understood nothing. In that first moment, like so many other men and women, I felt emptiness and abstract anger.

After a while, I reached for my wallet and found the piece of paper and the business card given to me by the prophet some time ago. The date he had predicted matched exactly.

I dialed New York and the prophet responded almost immediately.

"You may not remember me," I said.

"I do," he replied. "We met on Broadway and you were kind enough to buy me a cup of coffee. It was cold. I really appreciated it. I drank the coffee while warming my hands around the cup."

"How are you?" I asked. "I guess that's a very strange question to ask, considering what's happening..."

"No, it's fine. It's perfectly fine. And I'm doing well, thank you for asking. Quite busy, of course: informing people about the future."

"What is going to happen next?" I wanted to know.

"The war, as always. Two wars. One relatively short one, one long and terrible, which will ruin an entire country and kill hundreds of thousands of people."

"And then?"

"There will be another war, in the country that you know extremely well. And then one terrible disaster in Asia, an earthquake and Tsunami wave that will kill hundreds of thousands, maybe millions of people. Not only the quake, it will be followed by diseases, riots..."

"It sounds like you are predicting the end of the world," I said.

"Of course not. These things happen, you know. They always happen. Poor people will die. Poor people always die. Tens of thousands of them die every day. It's usually not so visible."

The prophet sounded calm, his voice as matter-of-fact as that of a weather forecaster.

"I'll call you again," I said.

"Please do. Nice talking to you."

Reiko watched me intensely.

"Who were you talking to?"

"A prophet," I said. "I met him in New York, during my last visit. He told me about this calamity, a long time ago."

"I thought you did not believe in such things," she said.

"I don't," I said. "But he made sense. And what he said really happened."

"So what will happen now?"

I shrugged my shoulders. I had no idea. "Nothing bad will happen to the two of us. As long as we stay here."

But the world was changing dramatically. There was no more doubt that democracy had died in the rich countries. People voted for morally corrupt clowns who were paid by anonymous companies and donors. Reiko and I began to follow the news again. People called us from all corners of the world – former colleagues, friends, relatives.

I had been invited to speak at two prestigious universities. I refused, unwilling to travel, not knowing what to say.

Professor Kohn had been giving a lecture at Tokyo University on the color of God. He called one evening from a loud bar in Yokohama, his voice hardly audible against the background noise.

"God is great!" he said. "There is no way anyone can compete with him. Because he doesn't exist he has no faults and no flaws, he makes no errors. All errors are made by us – people. He never intervenes. He never speaks. He never shows his color. If this is the case, as we all should know that it is, I am declaring his existence or nonexistence irrelevant!"

There were two wars, one following the other, and no real opposition to them. The empire became edgy and uncomfortable with its belligerent isolation in the world. But it went ahead anyway, full speed, ignoring the voices of those who demanded a different world.

In many poor countries, religions gained ground, becoming the main anesthesia for the poor, a straw to which to cling. In these miserable places, history was not taught. Teaching ceased to help people think, and instead commanded thoughts. Intellectual freedom was frowned upon, and was substituted by the medieval familial orders and religious terror. And in the rich world, the situation was not much better. Philosophy had become an outdated subject, locked behind the walls of a few elite universities. The poets fell silent. Alternatives disappeared. Rebels joined the middle class.

Mosques in countries like Indonesia now loudly broadcast sermons for hours, beating into submission those few who remained secular and true to their own perceptions of the universe. But in most of the rich countries, this Orwellian indoctrination had been performed too – by the mass media which gradually accepted its submissive role as a propaganda machine, serving anonymous corporate masters and boards of directors, instead of the public. Lies and clichés were developed and almost never challenged: current events were discussed in sheer ignorance, outside of accurate or even any historical context – the problems of western and south Asia, the Soviet Union, China, Cambodia, Rwanda, Africa north and south, the Americas, issues of finance and economics, climate change, and weapons of mass destruction, and on and on. Humanists had to shut up – or were rendered irrelevant. Social states in Europe and Asia were collapsing, one after another. Secular nations were disappearing. It seemed that only the fundamentalists had managed to survive and claim victory. Now they faced each other: market fundamentalists and religious fundamentalists. Both lacking compassion, both fanatical, brutal, and endlessly dull. Both aggressive and rough, lacking decency, warmth, kindness, even a sense of humor.

While this had all happened gradually for decades, now it felt that events were progressing at breakneck speed. The brave new world – a perfect dictatorship – had appeared to arrive.

47

We ate raw fish, drank gallons of green tea, made love several times a day. We talked and read books which we had never taken time to read before. Long books, nineteenth century novels, poetry. We listened to Xenakis, to Mahler, Shostakovich, to Russian romantics, to South African jazz. We rode bicycles all around the island, bathed in the hot spring, cooked the few same dishes that we both liked.

My wounds healed. Two scars remained but they were nothing more than that – small scars.

The wide world seemed far away, brutal and predictable, while we sheltered ourselves, created our own universe, kept a distance. I refused to question the morality of such behavior, I felt that I had already given enough, that now I had a right to live my own life, to enjoy simple pleasures, to wake up every morning next to the person whom I loved.

I sent a chunk of money to Lima, to pay utility charges for my apartment a year in advance. I transferred money to the maid, asking her to water the plants and flowers and to clean the dust once a week. Suddenly I had no responsibilities, no duties and no practical issues to take care of.

Then one morning our phone rang.

I heard a long pause, some noise, and then the distant voice of Felipe who was by now the Minister of Defense.

"It has begun," he said. "They are bombing the capital city. The entire border area is turning into a battle zone."

Reiko picked up the second line, her expression that of discomfort, and then fear.

"Karel," he said. "Would it be too inconvenient.... I mean, damn it, are you coming back?"

"I can't," I said. "For me, it's over. I don't want to return, Felipe. I don't write for the Globe, anymore."

"It's not about The Globe," he said. "We gave you honorary citizenship. It's now your country, too."

"I've never had any country that I consider mine. Not before, not now."

"A pity," he said.

"What's happening?"

"They bribed the army of the neighboring country, which immediately began terrorizing our border towns. We never retaliated. We brought it to the UN. We tried to avoid conflict. Three days ago, they burned two of our cities to the ground. We were forced to fight. We pushed them back. The US immediately accused us of starting a war with our neighbors. It accused us of attempting to spread revolution beyond our borders. Right now they are bombing our capital. They have two hundred thousand troops ready to enter our homeland."

"What are you going to do?"

"Fight," he said. "We'll fight any aggression."

"You will fight the United States?"

"What else are we supposed to do?" he asked. "Turn into another Salvador or Nicaragua? Take it in the ass and let them do it to our people?"

"I don't know," I said. "You can't win."

"No matter what we do, we will lose. At least we can try to defend what is ours."

"Call me in one hour," I said.

I searched the internet. There were confusing reports from all the major press agencies. Blurry, nothing concrete. The capital city was under attack. Intense bombing was destroying the infrastructure: bridges, power-stations, airports, and military installations. Washington had declared that it would not tolerate another Cuba in the Western Hemisphere.

Enormous anti-American demonstrations were taking place in all the capitals of Latin America. Members of the UN Security Council condemned the American attack, but the resolution was vetoed by the United States.

It was familiar, predictable. There was no escape, Felipe's revolution seemed doomed.

Then the latest news appeared on the screen and I read it in disbelief. The governments of two large South American nations had declared a state of emergency, mobilizing their troops. Their fighter jets had taken off, following a direct northern course –

toward Todos los Santos and the capital. Both governments declared that continuous attacks against the small and defenseless Latin country would be considered a declaration of war against all of Latin America. Two more governments joined in a matter of minutes.

Reiko was sitting next to me.

"What will happen now?" she asked.

"The US will not dare fight half the continent," I said. "It's that simple. If there had been similar solidarity twenty or thirty years ago, the world would be a different place by now."

"They may go all the way," she said.

Felipe called a few minutes later.

"Why do you want me there?" I asked.

"Because we need you. We need those few people who never sold out like whores," he screamed. "We need you to tell the story."

"What's happening now?"

"We declared total mobilization. Every house, every village will fight. We want freedom and democracy. Our own freedom and democracy. Unless they kill most of us, they will never take this place."

"Why are you doing it, Felipe?" I asked. "Why are you ready to risk millions of lives?"

"It's not us who is attacking, it's them."

"I understand. But we all know the new global rules of the game. We all know what may happen. Are you doing it for the sake of some ideology, for the sake of your own revolution?"

Felipe paused for several seconds. I heard him breathing at the other end of the line.

Reiko held the second receiver, while gazing through the window at the calm surface of the sea. I was surprised to see her smiling.

"I don't know," he said.

"You have to know, damn it!" I screamed at him. "That's not good enough, to say that you simply don't know."

"I'm not too good with words," he said.

"I've noticed that, but you should try to do a bit better, this time. You are deciding on the fate of more than 8 million people."

"I know," he said. "Then let me try..."

I continued to monitor the internet reports. The US bombers had left the national airspace, but the ground assault continued. There was heavy fighting in three border cities. Hundreds of thousands of women and children, carrying the few possessions they were able to salvage from their burning houses, were moving inland. Entire neighborhoods were reduced to rubble, villages leveled to the ground. New reports constantly appeared on the internet. Brazil and Venezuela withdrew their Ambassadors from Washington.

"Look," said Felipe. "This may not sound too beautiful, but this is what I feel right now. Fuck the revolution and fuck the ideology! I gave the order for each and every man to fight this invasion, because I don't want my people to starve anymore. Because I don't want them to labor for a pittance in some filthy foreign-owned factory, to be slaves to some small and corrupt group of native business executives who enjoy their company cars and villas while others eat shit and live in the gutter."

I realized that there was music, very subtle, filling the room. Reiko had probably inserted a CD into the stereo while I was speaking. I recognized *Quatuor pour la fin du temps* by Olivier Messiaen.

Felipe took a deep breath and continued: "I want my people to live like human beings. I want for them drinking water and electricity, decent hospitals and schools, roads and parks. And the way this world is arranged right now, unless we are free, unless we are able to defend ourselves, our people will never have anything at all."

There was a long sound of a siren coming from the port. Felipe lit up a cigar. I clearly heard him strike a match, and I recognized the sound of rough burning tobacco leaves.

Suddenly, Reiko put down her receiver. She stood up, walked around the room, came to me from behind. She put her hands on my shoulders, then hesitated for a moment.

"Go!" she said.

The entire universe collapsed, and promptly rearranged itself. Reiko, I thought, our room, our house and, behind two large windows, the endless sea and horizon.

"I'm coming," I said.

ANDRE VLTCHEK grew up in Central Europe and is a naturalized US citizen. Novelist, filmmaker, investigative journalist, poet, playwright, and photographer, he has covered dozens of war zones and conflicts from Bosnia and Peru to Sri Lanka, DR Congo and Timor Leste. He is the author of a novel *Nalezeny*, published in Czech. *Point of No Return* is his major work of fiction written in English and translated and published in French by Edition Yago. Other works include a book of political nonfiction *Western Terror: From Potosi to Baghdad* (translated into Turkish and published by Bilim + Gonul). Pluto publishing house in London recently published his provocative and critical book on *Indonesia: Archipelago of Fear.* Together with Rossie Indira, he is responsible for a book of conversations with the foremost Southeast Asian writer Pramoedya Ananta Toer, *Exile* (translated into Korean, Spanish and Indonesian). Non-fiction book *Oceania* (published by Expathos) is a result of his five years work in Micronesia, Polynesia and Melanesia and a damning attack against neo-colonialism in the Pacific. The plays *Ghosts of Valparaiso* and *Conversations with James* were translated into several languages including Spanish. He has collaborated with UNESCO in Vietnam, Africa and Oceania through various publications including fiction books *The Story of Ann* and *The Story of Moana.* Presently he is finishing writing his monumental political novel *Winter Journey.*

Andre is a Senior Fellow at The Oakland Institute. He writes and photographs for several publications worldwide, corporate and progressive, including Counterpunch, Z Magazine, Newsweek, Asia Times, People's Daily, China Daily, Irish Times, A2 and Asia-Pacific Journal (Japan Focus).

He produced the feature length documentary film about the Indonesian massacres in 1965 *'Terlena – Breaking of The Nation',* as well as the film on the biggest refugee camp in the world Dadaab *'One Flew Over Dadaab'.* His feature documentary film *'Rwandan Gambit'* is reversing the official narrative on 1994, exposing Rwandan and Ugandan plunder of DR Congo on behalf of Western imperialism. His Japanese crew recently filmed his lengthy debate with Noam Chomsky on the state of the world that is presently being made into a film and a book. He is working on several new documentaries in Asia, Africa, and Latin America. He frequently speaks at major universities, including Columbia, Cornell, Oxford, Cambridge, Sydney, Hong Kong, Auckland and Melbourne. Cofounder and Coeditor of Mainstay Press and Liberation Lit, he presently lives in Asia and Africa.

His website is: http://andrevltchek.weebly.com/

2194877R00199

Printed in Germany
by Amazon Distribution
GmbH, Leipzig